Starting Your Software Testing Career

A guide to finding your first role as a Software Tester, upskilling so you are relevant in the job market and succeeding as a Software Tester once you have landed a role.

Nicola Lindgren

Starting Your Software Testing Career

A guide to finding your first role as a Software Tester, upskilling so you are relevant in the job market and succeeding as a Software Tester once you have landed a role.

Nicola Lindgren

ISBN 978-91-527-2685-3

This is a Leanpub book. Leanpub empowers authors and publishers with the Lean Publishing process. Lean Publishing is the act of publishing an in-progress ebook using lightweight tools and many iterations to get reader feedback, pivot until you have the right book and build traction once you do.

Contents

Preface

I wrote this book with Software Testers at the start of their careers and people looking into moving into a role in Software Testing in mind. Experienced software testers who are looking for new ideas/ways to upskill will also benefit from reading this book.

Throughout the book, I share what I have learned throughout my software testing career. More importantly, I have interviewed dozens of people and collated their knowledge here for the reader. Please note that the opinions expressed in this book are the individuals' own and may not be representative of their employer.

There are a few people I want to thank, whose help made this book possible.

Thank you to Anna Makuchova, Elizabeth Zagroba, Jennifer Ann Lee, Phil Wong, Richard Bradshaw and Sebastian Holgersson - I really appreciate the feedback you gave me and how you helped me make sure this book had the target audience in mind.

Lastly, thank you to my husband, Andreas. Your support helped me not only start but actually publish this book.

Nicola Lindgren
Malmö, Sweden

Preface

Chapter 1: What is Software Testing? And Other Definitions

Before discussing how one starts a career in software testing, I think it's important to get an understanding of what software testing is, and more importantly what it isn't. This will be beneficial for you as you read this book.

I have also included other definitions that will help you follow this book. These definitions are not an exhaustive list of definitions you need to know as a tester (there are plenty of other books out there on that). However, I believe this list of definitions is a great starting point.

What is Software Testing?

The definition I most closely identify with, and more importantly, how this book will refer to software testing, is by Claire Reckless[1]

> *"The process of testing should be an investigation. We may not always know what the outcome will be but it's our job to uncover information which helps people make decisions."*

I most closely identify with this definition because over the course of my career, testing has always been an investigation. Sometimes

[1]https://www.ministryoftesting.com/dojo/lessons/so-what-is-software-testing

I knew what the expected result was, but not always - therefore I couldn't always "pass" or "fail" a test.

Next, let's go over what software testing is not.

Common Misconceptions Around Software Testing

You should only test against written requirements; to make sure the requirements are met.

A large aspect of software testing does involve testing against written requirements, but *it should not only be limited to testing against written requirements.*

When people write requirements, they do so with some implicit expectations - that they don't bother to write down.

You can read more about this in Chapter 9: Testing Against Implicit Requirements.

Software testing tries to prove that there are no bugs in a system.

This is impossible to prove.

You can prove the existence of bugs - by finding them. *But* you cannot prove the absence of bugs by thoroughly testing an area of software/ a feature/ some new functionality etc.

If you haven't found any bugs, the only thing you have proven is that *you* haven't found any bugs - not that the bugs don't exist. (This could be due to various reasons including lack of skill or lack of time.)

The best you can hope for, is to be able to claim that it is very unlikely bugs exist in the area you tested.

Going back to our definition of software testing - the fact that it is an investigation means that while it is unlikely bugs exist in the area you tested, we don't always *know* what the outcome will be.

A software tester is solely responsible for the quality of the product.

No, a team is responsible for the quality of the product.

A software tester's responsibility is to provide information about the product's state.

What is a Software Tester?

According to Techopedia[2]:

> *"A software tester is an individual that tests software for bugs, errors, defects or any problem that can affect the performance of computer software or an application."*

In reality, a software tester's job often goes beyond this. They are often expected to help improve quality practices (even without the word "quality" in the job title).

There are many ways in which you may hear someone refer to the software tester role, these include:

- Test Analyst
- QA (Quality Assurance) Engineer
- Test Engineer
- Software Quality Analyst
- Quality Analyst
- Quality Engineer
- Software Engineer in Test (This can depend on the company, in some companies, this may be more of a developer role, in other companies, this is more of a tester role)

[2]https://www.techopedia.com/definition/29845/software-tester

Test Cases vs Exploratory Testing vs Ad Hoc Testing

There are various interpretations of what exploratory testing is. For this book, this is the definition we will be using:

According to Deepak Parmar at Atlassian[3]:

> *"Exploratory Testing is an approach to software testing that is often described as simultaneous learning, test design and execution."*

Some argue that "Exploratory Testing" as a term, doesn't make sense, since testing in itself is exploratory. There are a lot of discussions in the testing world about the differences between "testing" and "checking". For this book - I will not go into this and stick to using the term "Exploratory Testing" when needed.

Exploratory Testing is often mistaken for Ad Hoc Testing and many testers say they are doing exploratory testing when they are, in fact, doing Ad Hoc Testing.

"Ad hoc testing is random, unstructured testing." (Source: Tricentis[4])

Test cases[5] are:

> *"A set of preconditions, inputs, actions (where applicable), expected results and postconditions, developed based on test conditions."*

[3] https://www.atlassian.com/continuous-delivery/software-testing/exploratory-testing
[4] https://www.tricentis.com/blog/exploratory-testing-vs-ad-hoc-testing/
[5] https://glossary.istqb.org/en/search/

What is Manual Testing?

> *"Manual testing[6], as the term suggests, refers to a test process in which a QA manually tests the software application."*

The alternative to Manual Testing is Test Automation, where automated checks are run against an application.

Test Cases, Ad Hoc Testing and Exploratory Testing are all types of manual testing.

What is a Test Suite?

According to ISTQB[7] (International Software Testing Qualifications Board):

> *"A set of test scripts or test procedures to be executed in a specific test run."*

What is Regression Testing?

According to ISTQB:[8]

> *"A type of change-related testing to detect whether defects have been introduced or uncovered in unchanged areas of the software."*

[6] https://www.browserstack.com/guide/manual-testing-tutorial
[7] https://glossary.istqb.org/en/search/
[8] https://glossary.istqb.org/en/search/

Regression testing is often done when you have introduced a change to an application. For example: You have fixed a bug, changed a feature or added a feature.

Often a team may need to do regression testing on an application to make sure that no unexpected changes have been introduced - this can be done with manual testing and/or test automation.

What is Smoke Testing?

According to ISTQB[9]:

> *"A test suite that covers the main functionality of a component or system to determine whether it works properly before planned testing begins."*

Another common term for this is "sanity test".

What is a Bug?

On projects, you may hear people refer to bugs as "defects". In software testing, there are many definitions of what a bug is.

In this book, the definition we use will be James Bach's[10]:

"Anything that threatens the value of a product"

In other words, anything that can negatively affect how a stakeholder can benefit from this product.

Unlike other definitions out there, this means you can find a bug that is not explicitly stated in the written requirements. You don't need to refer to written requirements to be able to raise a bug.

[9] https://glossary.istqb.org/en/search/

[10] https://www.satisfice.com/blog/archives/572

What is a Requirement?

"That which is required; a thing demanded or obligatory"[11]

Note that there is no mention of it being explicitly stated in a document etc.

There are two types of requirements in software development:

1. Explicit Requirements (what most people think of when they hear "requirements" - explicit requirements are explicitly mentioned, often in user stories, requirements documents etc.)
2. Implicit Requirements (What people expect, but don't feel the need to explicitly mention)

What are Implicit Requirements?

According to Product Plan:[12]

"Implicit requirements are features and characteristics of the product experience that customers will expect. In fact, without them, the market would view the product as incomplete."

In Chapter 9, we'll go into more detail on how to spot implicit requirements, the importance of testing against implicit requirements and how to test against implicit requirements.

[11]https://www.dictionary.com/browse/requirement
[12]https://www.productplan.com/glossary/implicit-requirements/

Functional Testing vs Non-Functional Testing

What is functional testing?

Here you are testing to make sure that the functions and features of the system work properly.
i.e. *What* a system does

What is non-functional testing?

Non-functional testing focuses on wider quality concerns such as performance, security and accessibility.
i.e. How *well* does the system do these things

Here are some examples of functional testing and non-functional testing:

Functional Testing	Non-Functional Testing
When a valid email and password is entered, a user is taken to the Profile screen	When a valid email and password is entered, a user is taken to the Profile screen within 2 seconds (Performance)
A user can Add a Product to Shopping Cart	A user can Add a Product to Shopping Cart using only their keyboard (Accessibility)

What is Testability?

In the December 2015 edition of Testing Trapeze, Maria Kedemo, Founder of Black Koi Consulting, describes it as:

> *"Testability is about how easy it is to test something. How easy it is to retrieve the information we need."*

Examples include:

- Observability - how easy for you is it to see what's happening? Good, informative logs are a way of making things more testable
- Understandability - how well is the application documented or self-explaining? Can you understand, what the application is supposed to do?

What Are Oracles and Heuristics?

What is an oracle?

> *"An oracle[13] is a mechanism for determining whether the program has passed or failed a test."*

Oracles are fallible - you can't *always* trust them, but they are a good thing to refer to when you want to know what expected behaviour is.

Examples include:

- Written requirements
- A person who can make decisions on what expected behaviour should be e.g. Product Owner, Client, Business Analyst

[13]http://www.testingeducation.org/k04/OracleExamples.htm

What is a heuristic?

> *"Heuristics[14] are principles which reduce the complex tasks of assessing probabilities and predicting values to simpler judgmental operations."*

Heuristics are also fallible. Like oracles, heuristics can't always be trusted, but they do give you a good idea of what to expect.

They are designed to help with decision making.

One thing to be aware of, is that the unknowing use of any heuristic can lead to systematic errors in thinking known as biases. Richard Bradshaw, CEO of Ministry of Testing and Sarah Deery, LearningBoss at Ministry of Testing point out that:

> *"Biases can have a detrimental impact on you and your testing. For example, under the availability heuristic, if you used a tool successfully in your last few projects, you might want to use it in the next even when there are more suitable tools available."*

In Chapters 8 (Test Cases vs Exploratory Testing vs Ad Hoc Testing) and 9 (Testing Against Implicit Requirements), I will go into some of my favourite heuristics.

What Are Feature Flags and Canary Testing?

Both are ways to manage risk when doing releases.

[14]https://www.ministryoftesting.com/dojo/lessons/software-testing-heuristics-mind-the-gap

What are feature flags?

According to Ian Buchanan from Atlassian[15]:

> *"Feature flagging (also commonly known as feature toggling) is a software engineering technique that turns select functionality on and off during runtime, without deploying new code. This enables teams to make changes without pushing additional code and allows for more controlled experimentation over the lifecycle of features."*

What is Canary Testing?

> *"Canary Testing is a way to reduce risk and validate new software by releasing software to a small percentage of users. With canary testing, you can deliver to certain groups of users at a time. Also referred to as canary deployments, incremental, staged, or phased rollouts."*

Source: Optimizely[16]

Agile vs Waterfall

Christina Ohanian does a great job in demystifying what Agile is, in this written interview.[17]

> *"Agile isn't about 'being fast' or speed. Of course, over time as you build your understanding around ways of working and processes within your teams, you can*

[15]https://www.atlassian.com/continuous-delivery/principles/feature-flags
[16]https://www.optimizely.com/optimization-glossary/canary-testing/
[17]https://nicolalindgren.com/2021/11/22/interview-with-christina-ohanian/

> *become more efficient and delivery of work can speed up, however, this from my perspective is a by-product of the emerging benefits of Agile ways of working.*
>
> *It's about understanding what to build for your customer. It's about being able to adapt to both internal changes in direction and external influences beyond your control. It's about smart and effective collaboration and communication with the people whom you are working alongside to build your product.*
>
> *Agile practice simply enables teams and organisations to get the right skills and expertise together, to have a focused direction and to satisfy customers through continuous delivery and regular feedback loops."*

If you were to compare the Agile approach to Waterfall, you would find that the traditional waterfall approach involves each discipline contributing to the project then "throwing it over the wall".

According to Guru99:[18]

> *"Waterfall Model is a sequential model that divides software development into pre-defined phases. Each phase must be completed before the next phase can begin with no overlap between the phases."*

What is an API?

API (Application Programming Interface) is a set of definitions and protocols for building and integrating application software.

[18] https://www.guru99.com/what-is-sdlc-or-waterfall-model.html

Think of an API as a contract

An API represents an agreement/contract between parties: If party 1 sends a request structured in a particular way, then this is how party 2's software should respond.

What is a Software Testing Technique?

According to Guru99:[19]

> *"Software Testing Techniques help you design better test cases. Since exhaustive testing is not possible; Manual Testing Techniques help reduce the number of test cases to be executed while increasing test coverage. They help identify test conditions that are otherwise difficult to recognize."*

Examples include:

- Boundary Value Analysis
- Equivalence Class Partitioning

What is Boundary Value Analysis?
As the name suggests, you are testing at the boundaries. It includes maximum, minimum, inside or outside boundaries, typical values and error values.

Often, a large number of errors occur at the defined boundaries.

An example of how you could apply this testing technique:

[19]https://www.guru99.com/software-testing-techniques.html

You are testing a bank transfer feature where the maximum allowed daily transfer is €1000 per day. To test this, you may then try a daily transfer of €1000, then €1001 or even €1000.01.

What is Equivalence Class Partitioning?
Here you are dividing test conditions into groups you see as equivalent.

An example of you applying this testing technique:

You are testing a date of birth feature, which only accepts the following format: DD.MM.YYYY. The date of birth entered would be the date of birth of the user. You may group the equivalence classes as follows:

Group Description	Dates
Date of birth in the future	12.02.2088, 14.11.3000
Date of birth too far in the past	11.01.1820, 08.08.1233
Invalid date of birth based on month	19.15.1998, 29.29.1956
Invalid format	19.11.89, 1.2.1989

Here, we are working with the assumption that any date in a group, will be treated in the same way as other dates in the group.

What is Shift Left (in testing)?

According to Alan Richardson on Devopedia:[20]

> *"Shift Left Testing addresses this by involving testing teams early in the process. Issues, be it in design or code, can be solved early on before they become major. In fact, shift-left is less about problem detection and more about problem prevention.*

[20]https://devopedia.org/shift-left

Shift Left doesn't mean "shifting" the position of a task within a process flow. It also doesn't imply that no testing is done just before a release. It should be seen as "spreading" the task and its concerns to all stages of the process flow. It's about continuous involvement and feedback."

Chapter 2: Gaining Skills Before (And After) Your First Role

In this chapter, I will focus on how to gain skills before you start applying for roles along with some personal recommendations on courses you can take and what skills you are likely to find useful in your career as a software tester.

What Skills Will You Find Useful as a Software Tester?

I'm going to break down this section into two parts, skills that (many) employers tend to look for and skills that you'll actually find useful in the day to day.

This might come as a surprise, but I've found there can be a significant difference between what skills employers tend to look for (or at least say they are looking for) and what skills you'll actually find useful in your role as a software tester. (This of course depends on the employer)

The skills you'll actually find useful in your role as a software tester are the same skills your employer will benefit from, but they might not realise this until after you've started working at their company.

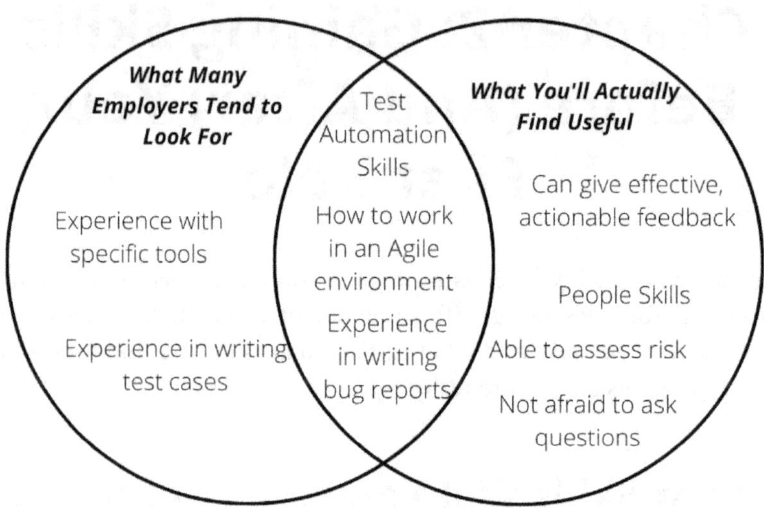

Skills Many Employers Tend To Look For

Test Automation Skills

It's becoming increasingly common for employers to look for test automation skills in future employees - even if the role isn't specifically for a "Test Automation Engineer" or something similar.

Often you'll see a requirement for this in the form of a specific test automation framework that they use at their company. For example: Selenium Webdriver written in Java or XCUI Tests written in Swift.

If they don't currently have a test automation framework set up at their company, they may just be looking for someone who can set it up.

If this is the case, you might not see something specific in the job ad like "Experience with Selenium Webdriver" or "Experience with writing XCUI tests" instead you may see something along the lines of "Experience in setting up a test automation framework".

Mid-Senior Level Needed

A company that is looking for someone to set up a test automation framework is likely looking for someone who is mid-senior level as it requires a fair bit of skill to do this.

It's a given that a candidate with Test Automation Skills can write code in the programming language they will work with, but unfortunately, it's not necessarily a given that a candidate knows what to automate and what not to automate.

Experience with Specific Tools

Another common tendency among employers is asking for experience with specific tools. These may be bug tracking tools, CI/CD (Continuous Integration/ Continuous Delivery) tools or other useful tools that they believe a successful candidate for the role needs.

An employer may ask for experience with a specific tool or with similar tools that serve the same or a similar purpose. For example: *"Experience with testing APIs using Postman (or equivalent)."* Other tools you can use to test APIs include Paw and SoapUI.

Tip

If you lack experience with the tool an employer explicitly mentions in a job ad, I strongly recommend you still apply for the role if you have experience using a tool that serves the same purpose, even if they don't mention "or equivalent".

The person writing the job might not realise there are other tools that serve the same purpose. It's the underlying knowledge that is important.

To increase your chance of getting an interview and not being automatically screened out because of your lack of experience with a specific tool, you can write something along the lines of: *"Experience with Paw, an API testing tool (similar to Postman).*

While there are bound to be differences between various testing tools e.g. various API testing tools, chances are your experience with one is likely to enable you to successfully pick up another.

For example: If you know how to test an API using Postman, you can reasonably assume you can learn how to test an API using an equivalent tool, fairly quickly.

How to work in an Agile environment
You'll probably see this requirement written as *"Experience working in an Agile environment"*

Agile

There are many interpretations of how to work in Agile, so your experience in Agile (including what you have read in books) may differ greatly from the company you apply to.

There's not a whole lot you can do about this, but be aware that you may be asked for your understanding of what Agile is and what it's like to work in an Agile environment, in the job interview.

Experience writing test cases and bug reports
This is pretty standard. But I would like to break this down into two parts; experience in writing test cases and experience in writing bug reports.

Experience in writing test cases

A lot of companies, including testers/test leads/test managers within those companies believe you can only test software by writing test cases in advance, then running those test cases once something is ready to test (i.e. once the developers have finished with a feature).

Testing using test cases is only one way you can test software. You have alternatives which I will go into in Chapter 8: Test Cases vs Exploratory Testing vs Ad Hoc Testing.

Experience in writing bug reports

An often underrated skill is being able to write clear, reproducible bug reports.

An employer may be looking for someone who has experience in writing bug reports but depending on who is doing the actual hiring and is involved in the decision-making process - the decision-maker might not know what a clear, reproducible bug report looks like.

In Chapter 7: Bug Reports, I will share how to write clear, reproducible bug reports.

Skills you'll find useful as a tester

There is a degree of overlap between these skills and the skills that employers tend to look for. This includes:

- Experience in writing bug reports
- Test Automation Skills
- How to work in an Agile environment

First, I would like to dive deeper into the previously mentioned skills before introducing new skills that you'll find useful as a tester.

Experience in writing bug reports
Not only you, but your whole team will benefit greatly if you can write clear, reproducible bug reports.

How you benefit:

- Gives you credibility in your team and helps you earn trust because bugs you raise are bugs that your team can reproduce
- You'll see that bugs you raise are actually fixed (since they can be reproduced)

How your team benefits:

- Time isn't wasted on trying to reproduce unclear bugs
- Bugs can be prioritised correctly for your team, so the most important bugs are addressed first

Test Automation Skills

While many employers are looking for someone with Test Automation Skills, many are looking for someone who has written Test Automation. However, they may not know what good Test Automation code looks like.

As a tester, you'll find it very beneficial if you know when you should and should *not* write test automation.

You may be asked to automate all the things! Or automate X% of test cases. In Chapter 10 - Test Automation, I will explain why these are dangerous goals to strive towards. I will share a few ideas for which cases you should and should *not* write test automation.

How to work in an Agile environment

Working in an Agile environment often means being able to adapt to change but more importantly having a different definition of who your "team" is.

In a waterfall setup, your "team" probably refers to your fellow testers, along with test lead(s) and/or test manager, you probably don't work directly with people in other roles such as developers, designers or business analysts etc.

In an Agile setup, your "team" probably consists of people in various roles including developers, designers, business analysts, product owners etc.

The distinction here is important because in an Agile setup, you may be the only tester in your team. While quality should be a team responsibility, if you are *the* tester in a team, you're probably going to be seen as the expert on how to test a new feature or new functionality.

Now I would like to introduce some new skills you would find useful as a tester:

Can give effective, actionable feedback

A tester is giving the team (often the developers) feedback on the feature or system that they have tested.

Often we expect/hope for people to gain some sort of value from our feedback, maybe we want them to know what a great job they did, or maybe we want them to know there are some areas of the feature which had quite a few problems.

If it's the last, then a tester should deliver the feedback in an effective, actionable way.

If you are expecting someone to take action (for example - to fix a bug), be clear about what you are expecting.

Even if you don't know exactly what the problem is, you can note down what you did to investigate the issue; what you tried to do etc.

People skills

A large part of our job as testers is working with people.

It's not hiding behind a computer and clicking away.

To be an effective tester, you need to be able to get along with people. One could argue that people skills are important for almost any role, but I think it's particularly important for testers because we often have to be the bearer of bad news.

Another key aspect of having strong people skills as a tester is that you need to be able to collaborate with others in your team. If you find yourself in a cross-functional team, working directly with developers, then you may work with them on tasks until completion.

Cross-Functional Team

A cross-functional team is a team that has different skill-sets needed to build features and/or apps. These almost always include: developers, designers, project leads. Often you'll also have testers in these teams (if the company has testers, keep in mind that some companies don't have dedicated testers).

Here are a few things I have learned, when it comes to dealing with (and connecting with) other people:

- Learn active listening.

Active listening[21] involves you listening without judgement and paraphrasing what you hear.

- Show appreciation.

If someone has helped you with something, (for example - given you access to certain tools), say thank you - don't just assume it was expected because it was part of their role.

- Be careful about interrupting

[21]https://www.verywellmind.com/what-is-active-listening-3024343#:~:text=Active%20listening%20refers%20to%20a,and%20withholding%20judgment%20and%20advice.

In some cultures, it's very disrespectful to interrupt. In other cultures, interruptions are more welcome.[22]

- Give credit.

This is similar to showing appreciation, but I think it also helps to give people credit in group situations. Were you impressed by a feature a developer built? Then mention it at standup the next day.

- Remember what people say, then follow up.

If someone says they are going to go bowling with their family this weekend, on Monday ask them how bowling was. (They'll be happy you remembered)

Able to assess risk

First and foremost, people should be testing the highest risk areas first, regardless of how much time they think they have.

By doing this, then the bugs that matter more, are more likely to be found first. Another benefit of this approach is that the amount of time given/allocated for testing can change - a risk-based approach mitigates that.

As much as we would like to dedicate "enough" time to testing, projects may run out of time and testing time gets cut (or you are forced to work overtime before a release).

You are then faced with a choice.

Which tests do I *not* run?

To answer this question, you need to know:
Which areas are the most risky? And which areas are less risky?

There are many factors that can make certain areas more risky, including:

---

[22]https://www.psychologytoday.com/us/blog/feeling-our-way/201504/the-communicative-advantages-interrupting

- What was rushed? Was there anything that forced your team to skip normal processes like code reviews or unit tests?
- Anything that touches a lot of different parts of the system?
- What do the developers seem to be unsure about? When you ask them questions about the expected behaviour, what are the developers not as confident in talking about?
- What will be the most used areas that the business will suffer greatly from, if it doesn't work?

What are code reviews?

It is the act of systematically convening with fellow programmers to check each other's code for mistakes. Developers aren't just looking for mistakes, but may also suggest to each other better ways to solve problems in their code.

What are unit tests?

This is a type of testing where individual components or "units" are tested. A unit may be an individual function, method, procedure, module, or object.

Not afraid to ask questions

You mustn't be afraid to ask questions, even questions that you may think are obvious or that everyone (else) knows the answer to.

Time and time again I've seen teams benefit from having testers ask questions, which sheds light on assumptions (including misunderstandings) that the team had.

Personal Recommendations for Courses You Can Take to Upskill

ISTQB Foundations

I'm going to address this first as many employers ask for it. While I've found a lot of other courses to be a lot more beneficial - I think it would be a shame to be screened out in the application process because you haven't taken a multi-choice exam.

Tip

Before taking the ISTQB Foundations exam and paying potentially hundreds or thousands of dollars to prepare for the exam, I suggest you look up the job ads for software tester roles at companies you are interested in.

Ask yourself, do these companies want someone with their ISTQB certificate?

If not, I wouldn't bother with this.

If so, there are ways you can prepare for this course and not spend a ridiculous amount of money doing so (the money you would spend would just be on sitting the exam itself).

You can buy the latest version of Foundations of Software Testing: ISTQB Certification[23] and study from there.

There are also a lot of online forums, YouTube videos and courses on Udemy[24], which you can use to help with your study.

In terms of how much time you need to dedicate towards preparing for the exam, this varies from person to person, some people could

[23] https://www.bookdepository.com/Foundations-Software-Testing-Dorothy-Graham/9781473764798

[24] https://www.udemy.com/

prepare for this in a few days of full-time study, others may need a few weeks.

BBST Foundations

If you don't have any experience at all in software testing, you may want to wait a year or two before taking this course,[25] as you won't have any real-life experience to apply in the course.

I do, however, want to highly recommend this course as I still use what I learned in this course over 8 years later.

In the meantime, you can learn still learn a lot by watching the videos and reading the course slides.

Rapid Software Testing Explored

Note: RST Explored is the latest version of the original class formerly called "Rapid Software Testing"

While I haven't personally taken this course, I know dozens of testers who have - and they have raved about it.

According to their site, the goals of the course are:[26]:

> *Apart from introducing the RST methodology, this class focuses on how to test a product when you have to test it right now, under conditions of uncertainty, in a way that stands up to scrutiny. It's about how to find important bugs before it's too late.*
>
> *A secondary goal is to help you think and talk like a testing expert, so that you can proceed with confidence and gain the credibility you need.*

Courses on Test Automation University

I have taken almost 20 courses on Test Automation University[27]. It's a free educational platform by Applitools[28]

---

[25]https://bbst.courses/bbst-foundations/
[26]https://www.satisfice.com/rapid-software-testing-explored
[27]https://testautomationu.applitools.com/
[28]https://applitools.com/

There are a lot of hardworking, talented instructors here, who have taken the time to share their knowledge with the software testing community.

Courses on The Ministry of Testing's Dojo
To access most of these courses[29], you'll need a Pro membership.

You can try out this platform with a free membership to see if you like what you see. You should be able to access a few courses for free or at least the first videos in some of the courses, with a free membership. (Unfortunately, you can't view any of the courses at all, unless you are at least logged in as a member.)

Gaining Skills with Crowd-Sourced Testing

What is Crowd-Sourced Testing?
Louise Harney[30] describes it as:

> *"Crowdsourced testing is the practice of sending out prototype software and products to a network of external testers instead of, or in addition to, testing internally. Crowdsourced testing companies have testers on their books from all around the world, with a number of different devices and operating systems, and people speaking a number of different languages. The networks can provide various different types of testing, including functional, usability, localisation or payments."*

Crowd Sourced Testing is a common way for testers to apply their skills while they look for their first role. It is also for testers (who

[29] https://www.ministryoftesting.com/dojo/courses
[30] https://harneytester.wordpress.com/2021/03/04/crowd-testing-friend-or-foe/

already have started their testing careers) to learn more about testing in a hands-on environment.

Gordon Crawford, Project Test Lead at bet365, shares how Crowd-sourced testing helped him up-skill:

> *"I found crowd sourced testing very valuable, I was at a point in my testing career where I had been a tester for a couple of years and knew I enjoyed the job but didn't know if what I was doing was good testing or if there were better ways to do it.*
>
> *I joined uTest mainly to compare the types of issues I was finding to other people and if they were finding more interesting problems then how were they finding those and could I do that the next time. It was also to see how other testers wrote up issues.*
>
> *I was working in a place where the domain knowledge was quite specific and most developers didn't have it so if I raised an issue there wasn't much push back to not fix it which led to me not writing the best bug reports.*
>
> *I was aware of this so by seeing what information other people would include/exclude, how they would frame issues and how to lay out a bug report it gave me good guidance for how to improve what I was doing at work."*

On his biggest takeaway from Crowdsourced testing, Gordon Crawford says:

> *"I realised that I was a good tester, even though were bits I could improve on - I was finding issues other people didn't which then went on to be fixed."*

Chapter 3: Getting Your First Job As A Software Tester

There are a few things you can do to get your foot in the door, but it can take a bit of time to actually land your first role as a software tester.

In this chapter, I'll share some possible paths you can take to becoming a software tester (including people's experiences on this), tips for applying for roles and some myths when it comes to applying for roles.

What Path Should You Take?

There are a few options regarding the very first step you can take.

1. **Join a company that has testers by using the skills you already have**

I've met a few people who became testers using this approach. This approach involves you using the skills/experience/background you already have to get the job – then later on try and go for a transfer into a software testing role.

Before doing this, I would do my research into making sure this company has transferred people between departments in the past and supported career shifts like this. (Some companies are great at promoting from within and giving internal people a chance at new roles – with the idea of developing them, other companies prefer to hire externally and only people with previous experience. Avoid the latter category of companies if you want to go with this approach).

Peter Pender, Development Manager at TouchBistro, explains how and why they have had people from their support team become testers at TouchBistro:

> *"The first two people who came through this path were very successful. Now we've had four or five people transfer from support to testing roles.*
>
> *They have valuable knowledge about the application, which helps them be effective testers. The only thing we need to teach them is testing fundamentals.*
>
> *We also know what we are getting - I can speak to their manager who can vouch for their work ethic."*

Depending on the role and the company, you may choose to ask about transferring between departments at your interview – either by talking about yourself specifically with regards to future opportunities in the company or by asking about how it works in general for others. If you are uncomfortable with being so direct, you can probably also ask around – see if you can talk to someone at the company to get an inside look as to how transfers between departments or changing roles at the company works.

2. **Do a Software Testing Education**

This isn't an option for everyone as you may not have this near you (and there might not be any distance-learning options), but this is a good approach to consider if you do have an education provider near you that offers a software testing course.

Some of the ones I know also offer internships giving students hands-on experience with the software testing world.

Some also have partnerships/already existing relationships with companies that can help you land your first role as a software tester.

Do your research, reach out to past students and find out what the course was like and more importantly what support was provided in helping them get their first role as a software tester. You'd be surprised by how generous people can be with their time and how they may want to help someone in your shoes as they, themselves, have probably had the same questions/concerns before they started.

To find past students, you can search for the education provider on LinkedIn[31], then on the View Company page, click on the Alumni tab – from there you can filter by year (to more recent years).

You can also filter by keywords/search terms such as "test" or "QA" (to filter out people who went to the same education provider but did something unrelated to testing).

Another way of finding past students is by asking in online discussion forums. Past students can reply and share their thoughts about the education they received.

Amanda Halvordsson, Consultant at Knowit, explains why she chose to do a Software Testing Education to start her software testing career:

> *"I studied various IT and tech subjects in Gymnasium/high school. When I finished, I knew I wanted to continue studying and to continue along that path. The details, however, were a bit more blurry. The only IT jobs I understood existed at that point were basically*

[31]https://www.linkedin.com/

> *different flavours of developer and support tech, so I figured I would end up studying and working with the former.*
>
> *I wanted an education that would allow me to transition into work prepared and confident. When I couldn't find that, I did what I did for high school when I ended up finding my tech and IT education – I broadened the search scope. After reviewing I believe every single education in Scandinavia that had anything to do with IT, there was one that really stuck with me.*
>
> *I hadn't realized prior that software testing was a valid career option, but the detective work and blend between technology and human aspects sounded perfect to me. The education was specifically tailored for this one job, allowing it to go into great detail and provide both theory and practical experience."*

David Dormvik, Test Consultant at House of Test, also did a Software Testing Education. However, he did a career switch. Here he shares why he chose to do a testing education to start his software testing career:

> *"I was at a point in my life where I was looking to quit my current job and do something completely different. I was looking into lots of different options. My brother in law was working as a test developer and suggested I'd find an education for software testing, as at that point there was a demand for testers in the region.*
>
> *Before that I had no idea that this was a career option. I was completely new to software development going into that education program."*

David Dormvik then goes on to explain how his internship (during his software testing education) also helped him find his first software testing role:

> *"While doing my internship as the last part of the testing education I had a list of companies/positions to apply to. I was quite methodical in keeping track of what step in the process I was in with each company. One of the positions was an opening at the same company where I was doing my internship but in a different department.*
>
> *I got great references from the department manager where I was doing my internship, however that raised questions from the hiring manager, "if he's so good, why aren't you hiring him?" It all worked out in the end. I think I went to one or two other interviews during the same period. I got hired just a few days before my graduation."*

Amanda Halvardsson had a slightly different experience when it came to finding her first role in software testing:

> *"Finding my first job was almost rudely simple. The education had a very cleverly placed internship module during the last few weeks. I managed to land myself an internship at IKEA through a guest speaker I had met earlier in the education. It was the first and only place I applied to, and after my simple Linkedin request, I had a message with an address and time for my first day of internship.*
>
> *Soon I was asked to join the project permanently as a tester, and as a consultant (like the majority of the project members), which I, of course, said yes to. All I needed to do then was find a consultancy firm, which was quite easy given my education and an already landed assignment in my pocket."*

3. **Upskill in your own time**

I think this would be the riskiest one but it is still possible to do it this way. I recommend you combine this approach with either 1 or 2 if possible.

There are plenty of online resources where you can upskill as a tester - see the Recommended Reading section for more details.

In terms of making the time to up-skill, I suggest that you:

- Give up/block social media and other time-wasting sites - or at least set limits on them so you can't use those sites for more than a specified period per day
- Apply limits to how much time you spend on your mobile phone - you'd be surprised by how much time you spend on your phone mindlessly scrolling
- Come up with daily, weekly and monthly goals - this can be in the form of a to-do list.

When it's come to making time for up-skilling in general (not just in the context of job hunting), I've found that personal circumstances can make this more difficult.

Since we had our children, I noticed that I have less personal time in general, and part of me was reluctant to give up any of this time to spend on up-skilling.

In terms of motivation, what helped me here was:

Plan ahead but manage expectations
I have only spent time on up-skilling after our children have gone to bed. I also let my husband know in advance that I want to have a night to myself (generally he's more than happy with this as it gives him time to game or up-skill as a developer).

But some evenings there is a lot of screaming and crying (from our children, not my husband).

While my husband does try to calm our children if I asked for some alone time - if they only want mummy, then I'll stop and try again another day.

Remind myself that any investment in myself will pay off, and it's something I have control over
Any skills I have learned can't be taken away from me. I have control over what I learn.

Listen to my body, and take breaks when needed - but overall aim for consistency.
That's why I suggest having monthly goals as well, sometimes I don't have the energy for a few days or a few weeks - but generally, over a month, I should be able to get a few things done.

Only learn things that interest me.
If the topic itself didn't interest me, then I looked for resources that presented things in an interesting manner so I *became* interested in it.

Remind myself of the why.
Why am I taking the time to up-skill in the first place?

4. **Networking**
A great place to start is Meetup[32] and see if they have any software testing meetups you can attend.

When asked if he would recommend networking as a way for people new to software testing, to land roles, Arjun Jhawar, Owner of AJ Consultancy Solutions, said:

> *"In today's society, which is dominated by social media, networking is critical.*
>
> *Knowing others in your business, or knowing others in the industry you want to get into, is, in my opinion, the most important part of landing good prospects."*

Ministry of Testing[33] also has software testing meetups all over the world, but these are also listed in Meetup.

---

[32]https://www.meetup.com/
[33]https://www.ministryoftesting.com/meetups

It's worthwhile looking into going to testing or software development conferences to go out and meet people. While many conferences cost thousands of dollars there are also plenty of more affordable ones (there are even free ones as well!).

When it comes to networking, my top recommendations for testing conferences are:

- The TestBash Conferences
- Agile Testing Days

Emma Keavney landed her first role in testing, because of her scholarship that paid for her to attend a conference:

Image source: Twitter

In my experience, there isn't a correlation between how much you pay to go to a conference and the value you get from it - so don't hesitate to book tickets to the free or very affordable conferences.

When looking into booking conferences, make sure you look at the conference program/schedule, to see if there are networking opportunities. Some conferences are great at providing plenty of opportunities for attendees to network with each other while others don't.

If you know anyone who has attended the conferences you are considering, I would ask them how the networking opportunities are for them.

You can also look up blog posts about past versions of these conferences to see what past attendees thought of the conference and what value they got from it.

There are some great online forums for networking – I recommend the Ministry of Testing's Club discussion forums[34].

In this discussion forum, they have a wide variety of topics that encourage networking including:

- Introduce Yourself threads
- What's your win for the week?
- Google hangout for testers

Lastly, when it comes to networking - I would like to recommend social media platforms such as LinkedIn and Twitter.

I've seen that people like to share interesting articles and pose questions to everyone on both platforms. Another benefit of being on Twitter is that having some idea of what people are talking about on Twitter lately might help make an interview conversation go more smoothly.

5. **Crowdsourced Testing**
I've been asked by multiple testers and seen quite a few people ask about Crowdsourced Testing as a path to becoming a tester.

I posted a tweet asking if I knew anyone who had started their testing career in this way.

Kristine Corbus, a former Software Quality Coach, replied:

[34]https://club.ministryoftesting.com/

Replying to @NicolaLindgren

Yes. I used it as a learning platform and sounding board. I was first time tester, working solo. I and what I did was so different that I thought I am going crazy. Crowd source testing normalised things and gave me confidence.

9:51 AM · Dec 7, 2021 · Twitter for iPhone

I asked Heather Reid, Community Boss at Ministry of Testing, why she signed up for Crowdsourced testing:

> *"My reasoning was two-fold, I used it to supplement my income and I used it to get experience in testing things that I couldn't get in the role I was in. I was very early in my career and wanted to get a broader range of experience to see where I might like to go with my career in the future."*

When asked if Crowdsourced testing helped her land a role, Aishwarya Vishwanathan, a Community Engineer at Applause, said:

> *"I started my journey as a freelance tester when I was in 10th grade. I've worked as a freelancer in almost all of the Crowdsourced software testing websites.*
>
> *Fast forward to 2019, I joined uTest as a crowdsourced tester. Later in 2020, I was promoted as an Academy Test Team Lead and this February, I got promoted again as a Community Engineer at Applause (Applause is the parent company of uTest). I work full time here and the best part is I enjoy what I do."*

Aishwarya thinks that Crowdsourced testing is a good option when it comes to starting one's software testing career:

> *"I would surely recommend Crowdsourced testing to everyone. You don't require any background In IT and anyone can get started easily. In fact, I introduced a lot of people personally."*

Meanwhile, Heather has a slightly different take on using Crowdsourced testing to start one's software testing career:

> *"It gives you a great range of experience both in testing and communication. For example, I got to test mobile apps which helped me to get my next role. I also had the opportunity to explore testing with geolocation which was really cool.*
>
> *There is a good and bad side to the experience it gives you in communicating with people though - which in hindsight probably prepares you quite well for working with different types of teams.*
>
> *In my first crowd testing role, there was no communication from the client. They had provided no information about the purpose of the product, any specific areas they would or would not like the crowdsourced testers to work on, any already known issues, etc.*
>
> *There were pieces of it that apparently weren't meant to work but they hadn't passed that information on. So if you logged a bug saying that the feature didn't work, it was rejected because they already knew this. At the end of the run then they docked all of the crowdsourced testers pay saying we had wasted their time. This was really disheartening because I felt that I'd worked really hard on the product.*

Contrast that experience with another project I was brought onto where there was a document explaining the purpose of the product, pages/tabs that don't or shouldn't work and known bugs.

If we had any issues, there was a point of contact in the company assigned to each group of testers and no financial risk was associated with contacting them. I only needed to contact them once because their documentation was really helpful. In this scenario, I felt that I got a fantastic all-around experience because I could really get into the product and see what good communication and testing looked like.

I would say if you are very early in your career, the first situation has the potential to put you off testing completely. Of course, you won't know which situation you're going into from the description of the project."

Applying for Software Tester Roles

Using LinkedIn

When it comes to applying for Software Tester roles, chances are you will not need to write a separate cover letter - the application process will probably only involve you uploading or sending in a resume.

To save time, you can use your LinkedIn profile to build a resume - all of the information from your LinkedIn profile is then turned into a resume.

Instead of creating a separate resume, you can enter all of your work experience, educational information, tools/technologies etc. into your LinkedIn profile - the added benefit of this is that recruiters can use your LinkedIn profile to approach you for potential roles.

Creating a Resume without LinkedIn
If you would rather create a resume without LinkedIn, you can use one of the many templates on Canva[35].
There are plenty of free templates to choose from.

A great thing about creating a resume without Linkedin is that you can tailor the Summary section to a role you are applying for.
You can also tailor the Experience section for a role - if you see that a role needs some sort of specific experience you have (e.g. in a tool you have used or other knowledge you have) then make sure you mention that and then expand on it.

Useful Skills to include in your resume
Sebastian Holgersson, Senior Consultant at an IT consultancy, shares what he is looking out for in resumes when reviewing them:

For testing in general:

- Curiosity and a willingness to learn
- An ability to look at software/hardware with a critical eye
- Being able to identify potential risk areas where you'd expect to find issues
- Being able to document issues systematically. Writing a clear reproducible bug report goes a long way.
- Knowing when to apply which testing techniques (For example: When would equivalence partitioning be applicable?)
- Domain-specific knowledge, e.g. for someone testing a web application:

For example:

1. *Understanding HTTP/REST, e.g. headers, request paths, JSON, request/response, CORS, cookies*
2. *Knowing how to use the developer console in the browser*

[35]https://www.canva.com/search/templates?q=resume

3. *Understanding how HTTP, JavaScript and CSS relate to each other*

For test automation:

- A reasonably solid grasp of at least one programming language (data structures, how to structure a project, code conventions, common libraries)
- Being able to look at an API specification and reason about what kind of tests would be used, as well as the ability to implement said tests
- Knowing how to work with common development tools is important when working with automation, and makes it easier for the tester to work independently.

Examples of such tools include:

- Git
- Docker
- CI/CD tools – Jenkins, Code Build, Github Actions
- Build systems (e.g. npm, maven)
- CLI (Command Level Interface) (e.g. bash)
- Some level of experience working with the cloud (AWS/GCP/Azure) can be very useful, depending on the domain
- Domain-specific tools and libraries, e.g. for the web domain:
- Knowing at least one frontend test framework (Selenium, Puppeteer, Cypress would all be fine) – preferably not an expensive enterprise tool.

Filling in the Experience section

I've helped review resumes and also screened resumes for Software Tester roles and noticed that there is often room for improvement in the Experience section.

When writing about your experience in previous roles, remember to also highlight any achievements you made in these roles, don't just write about what your tasks were.

Tip

You can structure your experience at each previous (or current) workplace using SBI (Situation Behaviour Impact) or STAR (Situation Task Action Result)

Here are some general guidelines:

- Ask a former colleague what achievements you made. Sometimes it's hard to be self-reflective, but the people around us may be better at noticing how we added value.
- Be specific with your results and achievements in the Experience section
- The results and achievements don't have to be massive, significant things - think about the smaller things you achieved as well.
- Were there any targets you met? Mention them.
- How did you add value to the company? Describe exactly how you did that

Here are some examples if you have a testing background, using the SBI structure:

- When I was working in a SCRUM team (Situation), I coached developers on how to test (Behaviour). As a result, my time spent testing new builds went down and releases went smoother (Impact).
- As a distributed test team on various projects, we struggled to find a way to share knowledge and collaborate regularly

(Situation). I set up a Testing Community of Practice at our company (Behaviour), which led to regular knowledge sharing sessions and an increased ability for testers to help other teams when a tester was off sick or on vacation (Impact).

Here are some examples if you have a testing background, if you choose to not use the SBI or STAR structure:

- Set up test process in our SCRUM team and guide developers on how to test
- Clarify requirements with our team to help prevent bugs from being written in the first place
- Started a Testing Community of Practice at our company, so that testers could network, collaborate and exchange knowledge regularly

If you don't have a testing background, you can use the guidelines and examples above to help you write about your experience.

When I was at university, I worked part-time as a Maths, Economics and German tutor.

Here are some examples of how I would describe my experience at the time (along with notes on how this can be linked to a testing career):

- Created study plans for my students to ensure they were ready for their exams in a timely fashion (demonstrates time management skills)
- Consistently helped improve my students' grades by at least 20% by explaining difficult concepts with analogies and tailoring homework to target areas of improvement (demonstrates communication skills)

Get someone else to look at your LinkedIn Profile and/or resume

This doesn't necessarily need to be done by a professional. Having another pair of eyes look at your LinkedIn Profile and/or resume will help pick up spelling mistakes, grammatical errors or things that just sound weird.

Make sure you ask someone who can be brutally honest with you. You don't want to ask someone who is afraid of offending you and doesn't bring up some concrete areas of improvement when there are things on your LinkedIn Profile and/or resume that can be improved.

I asked Gabbi Trotter, Software Testing Recruitment Team Lead at SearchabilityUK, what she is looking for when going through resumes:

> *"When it comes to hiring Juniors I focus on passion a lot. As you lack commercial experience we need to see your passion radiate through your CV.*
>
> *Ideally I want to see a strong cover note or opening statement on why testing, and why you think you'd suit this job, e.g transferable skills. Also, it's very hard to secure a Junior/Entry level role as competition is high, so please consider online free courses/resources you can complete and put on your CV to stand out.*
>
> *Things such as Test Automation University, reading MOT (Ministry of Testing) articles, attending Test Meetups or even trying your hand at freelance testing via UberTesters[36]. I don't think a degree is necessary and some of the best testers have come from totally different backgrounds such as retail or customer service."*

Sebastian Holgersson also recommends writing a cover letter:

> *"Cover letters are quite important when you're just starting out. It is a good place to discuss why you've*

[36]https://ubertesters.com/

decided to go in this direction, what your goals are, what you think you'd need more experience with, etc."

Meanwhile, Adelle Medalla, HR Officer/Talent Acquisition at a bank, is looking for something slightly different when going through resumes:

"Maybe a candidate can be very impressive if he/she has knowledge in multiple tools. Some QA Testers only know Manual Testing. While another candidate who knows both Automation and QA Testing may be a better fit for the role. Also if they have knowledge in other IT skills, like knowledge in database or network security."

Sebastian Holgersson describes some warning signs he has seen in resumes:

"I'd often see resumes where the candidate would list high levels of experience in several dozen tools, languages and techniques, only to struggle in the interview as they only had very limited experience with some of them. An honest description of your skills makes it easier for interviewers to ask the right questions and match your skills to their requirements."

According to Sebastian Holgersson, very long resumes aren't a good idea either.

"Formatting and highlighting key experience makes it much easier for a recruiter to read and understand your resume. It's also important to keep the overall length down, as a recruiter is more likely to miss things if your resume consists of several pages of densely-packed information."

Here are some ideas on how to make your resume stand out, in a positive way:

> *"A good CV is one that quickly shows what skills you have."*
>
> *"It's best to highlight the technologies you personally used, what role you had, what you achieved in that role etc. Bullet lists with a few key points per project go a long way."*
>
> *"If you have very little experience, highlighting personal projects is probably the way to go. GitHub repositories with a few simple-ish demos that you personally have created will be very useful. If you're not aiming towards test automation, crowdsourced test platforms are a good way to get practical experience that can look good on a CV."*

Interviewing for Software Tester Roles

The questions you may be asked in an interview will vary greatly from company to company. An important factor that will also influence what you will be asked is if you are interviewing for your first role as a software tester (and the company knows you lack experience) or if you are interviewing for a software tester role and the company expects you to have some work experience already.

Peter Pender shares what he is looking for in an interview, when hiring testers:

> *"One of the hardest skills to teach is the ability to calmly and factually explain a situation. This especially applies to software testers as they need to communicate*

> *with developers when things are broken. While most developers are receptive to feedback, there are times where it's very valuable to have this as a skill.*

Sebastian Holgersson describes how he is looking for people to show their testing skills in an interview:

> *"What I've tried to move towards has been a fairly practical example, and focusing on a discussion without any right or wrong answers. This could be something like testing a calculator application. How do they approach it?*
>
> *A good tester would probably fairly quickly be able to (intuitively or through some process) figure out some approach for how to measure the quality of the application.*
>
> *I would probably hope for some experimentation where the basic functionality of the interface is tested, and some sense of where you'd expect to find issues ("1+1=" will probably return 2, but "1/0=" could be interesting. What happens if you try to enter really large numbers? What happens if you try to enter letters or special symbols?)."*

For a test automation role, the above would apply, but there are a few more things Sebastian Holgersson would be looking for in an interview:

> *"I'd want to see some ability to program... we might look at some code see if they can understand what it does and how it does it.*
>
> *I am not a huge fan of live coding, since the tests are usually not very realistic, but reading and understanding code is easier to test and to discuss. Another possible*

> *test could be something like looking at a failing test, and trying to determine whether something is wrong with the test or the SUT (Software Under Test)."*

Here are some general tips for interviewing for software tester roles:

1. **Take your time when answering questions**

There is no need to start talking straight away when you are asked a question. Feel free to take a moment to think about what you are going to say before you open your mouth.

This is easier said than done.

But I've found this to be extremely valuable.

When interviewing candidates, I've noticed that nerves can make someone just start talking about what first came to their head.

If they only took the time to pause before answering the question then they could come up with answers that reflect their true ability and/or experience.

Phil Wong shares a tip for people who are nervous or aren't sure how they come across at interviews:

> *"Film yourself doing a 'mock interview'. No one is watching you apart from yourself and you can watch it back to assess yourself. Better yet, maybe ask a fellow tester to be the interviewer.*
>
> *Shy? Use a voice recorder instead."*

2. **Even when not asked for examples, feel free to provide examples**

Even if an interview question doesn't explicitly ask you to provide an example, if and when possible, I suggest you try and incorporate an example. This shows that you know what you are talking about and that you have experience in what you claim to have experience in.

3. **Prepare a list of questions to ask at the end of the interview.**

A useful tip I picked up from a past colleague is to write down the questions and bring them with you to the interview. By doing this, you ensure you won't forget what you want to ask.

I suggest you have at least 4 or 5 questions prepared. The answers to a few of them will probably be already covered during the interview and it's wise to have at least one good question to ask at the end.

Here are some suggestions for general questions you can ask at the end of an interview:

- What are the tasks I would do on a usual day or week?
- What does the onboarding process look like?
- How much freedom for decision making do testers in the team have? Can we decide how we test or is that dictated already?
- Do you have any concerns about my application or my suitability for this role?
- Who would I be working most closely with?
- What management style does my manager/the person I would be reporting to have?
- How can I develop in my role? What opportunities are there for career growth?

Here are a few more suggestions from Elizabeth Zagroba's article How To Interview Like A Tester:[37]

Questions for an HR person or any first interview

- What does the interview process look like going forward?
- How long has this position been open and when are you trying to fill it?

[37]https://www.ministryoftesting.com/dojo/lessons/how-to-interview-like-a-tester?s_id=12232999

- How did this position become available?

Questions for your future boss

- How will my work be evaluated?
- What has been a struggle for the team lately?

Questions for a teammate

- What drew you to this job and what do you like about it?

Questions for a C-level executive

- How do you measure success?
- How does my team fit into the wider company strategy?

4. **Make sure that the questions don't just reflect what you want to know, but also that you have done your research into the company and the role.**

Here are a few ideas on how to go about this:

- Do they have a company blog or even better, an engineering blog you can read?
- Reach out to people already at the company, and ask them what makes their company special, then incorporate that into the interview
- Is there anything unusual about how they go about software development? Ask them about this

5. **If you do not get an offer, ask for feedback so you can learn from it.**

This can be useful as you may not have the self-awareness to know what you could improve on in the future - being told exactly why you weren't picked for a role can better prepare you for other roles.

Also note, that sometimes this is out of your control. A company might have decided to promote from within, and already had someone internal in mind when they interviewed candidates.

Another possible, common explanation is that someone was better suited to the role. There isn't anything you could have done better (as your interview had best reflected your skills and personality)

Managing Expectations

It's important to manage expectations when it comes to applying for software tester roles. Adelle Medalla shares a bit of perspective from the recruitment side:

> *"For example, when we need someone with automation experience, Hiring managers would require someone who already has experience in using the tool.*
>
> *We are also considering salary and experience of the candidate. If the vacancy would only require for a tester who has 3 years experience but is already expecting a salary equivalent to a manager, we have to look for other candidates who can fit the salary bracket that we can offer."*

Some Myths When It Comes to Applying for Roles

Apply for all roles that you can
To a certain extent, you should cast your net wide, and apply to

multiple roles at different companies, but I strongly suggest you don't spread yourself too thin. Remember: Quality > Quantity

I shouldn't apply if I don't meet all the requirements listed in the job ad

Having been on the receiving end of going through resumes and also later finding out who was successful in actually getting the roles - I assure you that companies don't always insist on 100% of the requirements being met.

Tip

Even if you don't match all of the skills/requirements listed in the job ad, apply anyway if you believe you can do the role.

The purpose of a job interview is for you to impress the company

The purpose of a job interview is for you and the company to evaluate each other to see if you are a suitable match.

The company is interviewing you and trying to see if they want you and should make an offer. You should also be interviewing the company to see if you want to work there; if you want to spend a large chunk of your waking hours helping them reach their company goals.

To a certain extent, you are trying to impress the company as you want them to see what you have to offer (and it's great to have a job offer you can decide whether or not to accept).

The company should also be trying to impress you.

This doesn't just apply in the job interview itself, but throughout the job application process.

You shouldn't have to wait several weeks after an interview for a reply nor should you be ghosted by a potential employer at any stage during the whole process.

Chapter 4: What Does a Typical Day Look like?

What a typical day looks like varies greatly from company to company, even from week to week in the same project.

How one's day looks can also depend on what you are testing. For example: Testing smartwatches or revolving doors is probably fairly different to testing a banking app. (i.e. You can have a very different experience testing hardware compared to testing software)

Here, I will share with you what a typical day has looked like for me in different work environments and will share the context with you.

I will also share which aspects I liked and didn't like in each work environment.

Large Waterfall Project

Context:

- We were integrating multiple government systems
- Over 100 people on the project
- I sat with a team of other testers
- Working towards one big release
- We wrote test cases, based on a requirements specification that was fairly fixed - any changes made to requirements had to go through a Change Review process that involved multiple stakeholders
- No direct access to the developers

- Designs were not available
- It would take more than 6 months for builds to become ready for testing

While I'm waiting for a build to test

- No regular daily team meetings, we had weekly meetings as a test team
- Initially reading a lot of documentation and getting familiar with the requirements
- Once I felt I understood the requirements, then would start writing test cases using the Test Case Management Tool
- Get reviews on the Test Case Management Tool from others in the test team including the Test Lead
- Once the test cases were written, sit around re-reading documentation until the build was ready to test

When our test team has received a build to test

- Regular daily team meetings as a test team
- Execute the test cases which we wrote earlier
- Write bugs in the Bug Tracking Tool
- Bug severity was determined by the testers, but bug priority was determined by regular defect triage meetings that only the Test Managers were a part of

The day of a release

- Since our test team was so removed from the actual release process, there wasn't any special tasks we had to do.

What I liked about this work environment:

Working with and sitting beside other testers meant it was very convenient to ask for feedback from them and bounce ideas off each other.

What I didn't like about this work environment:

Finding issues so late in the process and realising that it would be a rather long time for me to be able to retest issues as it had to go through two other testing phases first. I was in the User Acceptance Testing team. The other two testing phases were System Test and System Integration Test.

Co-Located Scrum Team Working With Multiple Releases Each Day

Context:

- We worked on various features in a specific product area
- 8 people in a cross-functional Scrum team
- Developers could only have branches open for a maximum of a day, if branches were open longer than this, they were considered too big and were expected to be broken down into multiple branches (We wanted to keep changes small)
- Feature flagging and canary testing were utilised often
- There were multiple pushes to Production each day
- Business Analyst and Product Owner wrote user stories based on feedback from customers and the customer support team.
- Backend had a tendency to be ready about a week before the frontend, so would often test the API first, then a week later the frontend with the backend built-in (wasn't mocked)

Each and every day, as we do multiple releases a day

- Daily 15min stand-up in the morning
- Aside from the standard "What did we do yesterday, what will we do today and any blockers", we also discussed what's going out to Prod each day
- Talk to the senior backend developer and senior frontend developer in the team to know what's ready for test and what's coming up in the next few days
- I would pair with the developers as they would show me what is about to go out to Prod either later today or later in the week
- I would work on mind-maps for testing upcoming features and share this with the developers to get their thoughts
- I would pair with other testers from other Scrum teams when I got builds ready for test or to talk them through what I tested, to get their feedback

What I liked about this work environment:

The fast pace - I learned so much in this team because we were always very busy.

What I didn't like about this work environment:

At times it was hard to pair with other testers when everyone happened to be very busy in their teams.

Co-Located Scrum Team Working With 1-2 Releases Each Month

Context:

- We worked on various features in a specific product area
- 12-14 people in a cross-functional Scrum team
- Feature branches would often be open for 1-2 months
- 1-2 releases a month
- Manual/hands-on testing and writing test automation code - roughly 60:40 time split overall between manual testing and writing test automation, but this would vary depending on how far we are from a release.

About 1-2 weeks before a release

- Daily 15 minute stand-up in the morning which covers the standard "What did we do yesterday, what will we do today and any blockers"
- Reach out to the developers directly in the team to know what's ready for test and what's coming up in the next few days
- Focus on testing for features that are in the next 1-2 weeks
- Write test automation code for any features that are in the main branch

The day before a release

- Daily 15min stand-up in the morning which covers the standard "What did we do yesterday, what will we do today and any blockers"

- Double check with everyone that we have what we need and the timing of when we plan to push to Production
- Go back over my testing notes and what's covered in the release to make sure there's nothing missing

The day of a release

- Generally calmer than the day before a release, as we should be ready and don't try to squeeze in last-minute changes
- Daily 15min stand-up in the morning which covers the standard "What did we do yesterday, what will we do today and any blockers"
- Sanity testing to make sure release went well
- Focus on preparing tests for upcoming features that are not part of the day's release
- Hopefully celebrate!

What I liked about this work environment:

The split between manual testing and test automation - the variety of what each work week offered really appealed to me.

What I didn't like about this work environment:

The team was too big for my liking - it meant sometimes things fell between the cracks because of all the communication channels.

Chapter 5: How and Why You Should Find a Mentor

Looking back on my career so far, one of the things I'm most grateful for is having had some inspirational, helpful mentors since near the start of my career.

I'd like to share with you the story of my first mentor.

> About a year after I started my testing career, my boss left the company. We stayed in touch by meeting up for lunch or coffee about once a month. We also co-started a testing meetup together along with two others.
>
> One of the things I fondly look back on is that she was one of the first people who believed in me - actually saw something in me. Later on, I remember thinking about switching roles and there were a few companies that I was interested in.
>
> But I started to doubt myself because I was thinking *"Why would these awesome companies hire me? There are plenty of better testers out there, why should I even bother applying?"*
>
> She reminded me of what I had to offer, and why a company would have been lucky to have me.
>
> I applied for the one I was most interested in and got the role - all because she believed in me (I wouldn't have even tried otherwise).

What is a Mentor?

According to Indeed,[38]

> *"A mentor is an individual who acts as an advisor or coach for a less experienced or advanced mentee, providing expertise and professional knowledge from a more experienced perspective."*

I quite like how Bob Proctor[39] puts it:

> *"A mentor is someone who sees more talent and ability within you, than you see in yourself, and helps bring it out of you."*

Put simply, a mentor is someone you can learn a lot from as you start your career in software testing.

Benefits of Having a Mentor

There are many benefits to having a mentor, some of the ones I personally have had include:

- Discussing problems about work to get ideas on how to resolve them
- Discuss ideas and how I can implement those ideas at work
- Advice around salary negotiation (both for new and existing roles)
- Getting an idea of what's out there in the software testing world - since a mentor is more experienced, then my previous mentors have helped me gain perspective on whether what I am experiencing at work is normal or not

[38] https://www.indeed.com/career-advice/career-development/what-is-a-mentor

[39] https://www.goodreads.com/quotes/4473069-a-mentor-is-someone-who-sees-more-talent-and-ability

How to Find a Mentor

It can be hard to formally find a mentor. To start with, I would like to state that a mentoring relationship may begin naturally without you actively seeking one (this is actually how a few of my past mentor-mentee relationships came about).

Past colleagues who I admired and respected became my mentor over time, and then after a while I realised - that a mentor-mentee relationship had formed.

According to Harvard Business Review[40], while 76% of people think it's beneficial to have a mentor, only 37% actually have one.

This is often due to a fear of rejection - so people don't even bother asking.

If you want to actively look for a mentor, here are some ideas on how to go about this:

Ministry of Testing - Looking for a mentor discussion thread
Here[41] you can write a short post on who you are, what you think you need help with, where you want to get to and how to get in contact with you

Approach a colleague
If there is a colleague you would like to have as your mentor, then seek them out for advice - have coffee with them etc.

Take the opportunity to get to know them and you may find that you don't need to explicitly ask someone to become your mentor for them to become your mentor. Of course, if you feel uncomfortable with this - you are welcome to have the discussion.

Ask around to get the word out
I've seen people post on Twitter and LinkedIn saying they are

[40] https://hbr.org/2021/03/whats-the-right-way-to-find-a-mentor
[41] https://club.ministryoftesting.com/t/looking-for-a-mentor/65

looking for a mentor, then others would share the tweet or post - and then tag people they think would be suitable.

In the past, I've also connected people that I knew were looking for a mentor, with people I thought were suitable. After talking to these people who wanted a mentor, I realised that I couldn't offer them what they were after, *but* I knew someone who would be a good match, so I connected them.

A mentor doesn't need to be based in the same city as you
In today's society with great communication tools, you can have a mentor who is based in a different city (or even a different country).

How to Have a Successful Mentor-Mentee Relationship

Communicate expectations clearly
I think it's good to be on the same page with your mentor on how this mentor-mentee relationship will look.

While I think it's your mentor's responsibility to communicate this, if your mentor doesn't do this - then feel free to ask about the following:

- How often should you meet?
- What do both of you hope to gain from this?
- What expectations does your mentor have of you?
- What expectations do you have of your mentor?

A successful mentor-mentee relationship doesn't have to go on forever
There's nothing wrong if a mentor-mentee relationship has run its course.

At some point, it may naturally come to an end. I don't think either one of you needs to formally end things - chances are you'll both realise it's time to move on.

Share your goals
If you talk about your goals from the beginning of the mentor-mentee relationship, then your mentor can help you keep on track.

Make sure your goals are SMART.

- Smart
- Measurable
- Achievable
- Realistic
- Time-bound

Mentoring vs Sponsorship

People can confuse mentoring for sponsorship - both are very beneficial for one's career, but they are completely different things.

I've benefited a lot from having mentors, but also from having people sponsor me. Though at the time, I didn't know that this is what they were doing.

Sponsors have helped increase my visibility at organisations, which in turn - resulted in more opportunities in my career.

Here are a few examples of the opportunities that have opened up to me because of sponsors:

- Been recommended for projects
- Been asked to deliver presentations internally
- Been invited to speak at conferences

What is sponsorship?

According to Janice Omadeke, at the Harvard Business Review[42]:

> *"The mentor can become an actual advocate for their mentee. In this capacity, the mentor is now a sponsor and the mentee is a protégé.*
>
> *Now the sponsor is doing more than just sharing experience and knowledge. Because the sponsor has come to feel personally invested in the advancement of the protégé, the sponsor expands that person's visibility within the organization, models self-advancing behaviour, and directly involves the protégé in experiences that will provide opportunities for career advancement."*

Being sponsored by someone can be extremely beneficial for your career. By having a sponsor, you have someone advocating for you and actively helping your career.

Lena (Pejgan) Wiberg, Engineering Manager at Mentimeter, shares how she has helped someone's career by being their sponsor.

> *"One of my direct reports was really frustrated and wanted a change. She had been invested in a lot in the past, including a very expensive, time-consuming training in Project Management.*
>
> *She had been applying for a few internal roles and felt stuck and worried the investment would be wasted.*
>
> *We did have an open role at the time, but she didn't dare to apply for it. The role was a replacement for a very experienced person and was phrased in an intimidating way - aimed at very senior profiles. The role had already*

[42]https://hbr.org/2021/10/whats-the-difference-between-a-mentor-and-a-sponsor

been published externally, meaning she would have to compete with external candidates.

I could clearly see this was a win-win situation:

- *My report would get a chance to switch to a role with a better career progression in the safety of a well-known environment*
- *I would get to keep a valuable employee*
- *The company would get a hungry new project manager with lots of knowledge about the business while being able to shape them in the way we wanted to work.*

I had long discussions with my boss (the hiring manager) on why I believed in her, how we could shape the role to fit and which types of projects we could give her, as well as how I would support and mentor her.

In parallel I had long discussions with my report on the same topics: why I believed in her, coaching on how to pass that type of interview process and how there would always be a place to fall back on in my group/her old team if it didn't work out.

In the end - she applied, was allowed into the process and fought head to head with some really cool candidates. She got the job, we got to keep a great asset and she blossomed into a fantastic project manager. I am extremely proud of her.

Chapter 6: What I Wish I Knew in My First Year of Testing

Expectations vs Reality

Perception of quality

My understanding of what quality was, was similar to perfection - I thought all (known) bugs had to be addressed before you went live. Bugs were something that hurt the quality of the software. As time passed, my understanding of quality and "good enough" has changed. Now I don't only focus on bugs, but mainly on the value that can be provided to the stakeholders.

With time, I've realised that there is nothing wrong with "good enough".

Instead of aiming for perfection, the question I am trying to answer with testing before we release software is:

Is it good enough yet?

Agile

I've been on a lot of 'Agile' projects. I've found that some companies believe they have Agile projects just because they are doing a daily stand-up (while there is some value in running daily stand-ups to make sure that everyone is on the same page, I've found it can be hard to focus when the daily stand-up can run up to 30-45 minutes long).

I can't help but think that many companies and a lot of people have started to throw around the term "Agile" but not everyone understands its meaning.

While I have worked on some projects that implement a lot of the fundamentals from the Agile Manifesto, they are, however, outnumbered by the projects I have worked on that only claim to be Agile.

The purpose of testing

Even something as simple as why we test software is something that I haven't always agreed on, with the people I have worked with. It never occurred to me that my understanding of the purpose of testing would not be the same as other testers (let alone other people on a project).

To me, it was a given that we would at least have a shared understanding of what testing is supposed to achieve.

But I was wrong.

There are multiple interpretations of the purpose of testing.

My interpretation: We test software to get a clear picture of the state of the software.

I quite like Anne-Marie Charrett's analogy, which I heard at Agile Testing Days 2018.

> *"Software testing is the headlights. Quality is the journey. Business Outcomes is the Destination."*

Here are a few purposes of testing I have come across, which I disagree with, along with reasons why:

- To find all the bugs - you can't ever KNOW that you have found all the bugs as it's near impossible (if not impossible) to prove that something does not exist.
- Testers should care about all bugs equally - testers should focus on the bugs that matter to stakeholders.

Phil Wong, Test Engineer at Kin + Carta Europe, shares his experience reporting bugs at the start of his career, before he realised he should focus on the ones that matter to stakeholders:

> *"I must've reported over 30 tickets that were never prioritised or touched in the end.*
>
> *I quickly realized that it's worth focusing my time on the bugs that matter to stakeholders."*

- To improve the quality of the software - testing in itself doesn't improve the quality of the software, but if testing is done well it can give your team a good idea of what needs to be improved.

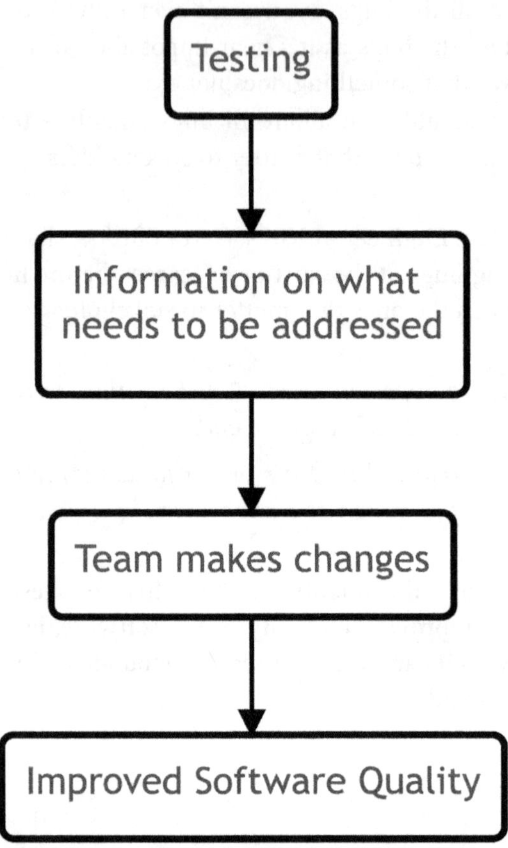

Get Involved With The Testing Community

How I discovered the testing community
At my first company, I worked with a few people who were involved with the testing community – it is through them I discovered that it existed. There were also a few people at the company who organised a testing meetup in Wellington, New Zealand. Later my

former mentor and two other women started a testing meetup in Auckland, based on the model that was done in Wellington.

Note: The meet-ups would have a 20-minute experience report (where someone shares their experience on something) and then this is followed by a facilitated discussion where everyone can share ideas with each other (not just direct questions towards the speaker).

How I have benefitted from attending meetups (and seen others benefit)

- *Discovery of new testing tools and how they are being used*

By attending meetups, I was able to listen to others share their experiences on what testing tools they used and why. They would also often share why they chose the tool and any struggles they had.

- *Expand understanding of how testing is/can be done*

If you only work at one company for a long time, then your understanding of how testing can be done is probably fairly limited. From what I have seen, testers who don't try to see what's out there and expand their understanding on testing, might not even realise that their understanding is limited.
By attending meetups you'll get to see what other testers are doing and how they are solving problems etc.

- *Networking*

You get to meet new people. I also know a few people who got jobs based off people they met from attending meetups.

Arjun Jhawar, Owner of AJ Consultancy Solutions, shares his experience on networking to find a role:

> *"When I landed in New Zealand, I found myself alone in a whole other world with a completely different culture and traditions, including work-related ones. I didn't see any hardcore 9 to 5 workers here. I also felt the need to develop new industry acquaintances because one of the things I've found difficult here is being informed of and knowledgeable about new roles that are available.*
>
> *As a result, I began to use platforms like LinkedIn much more than I did in India. In 2013, LinkedIn wasn't as popular as it is now, but it still helped me connect with the appropriate people in New Zealand. I also went to other company offices unannounced, requesting volunteer work, which never worked out, but it provided me experience opening up and speaking with people, which I lacked in my former life as an IT professional in India.*
>
> *I signed up for a website called meetup.com, which listed numerous social activities taking place around one's present location.*
>
> *That's where I met Peter Pender, who was working as a QA Manager at a company in Auckland called Vend at the time. He liked me for some reason and offered to interview me for a QA position at their company. The rest, as they say, is history."*

Peter Pender, Development Manager at TouchBistro, gives a bit of insight into why he's enjoyed going to meetups and meeting potential employees there:

> *"For junior roles, if people are going to these meetups, they are either trying to learn something new or they are looking for a role - sometimes both."*

How you can get involved with the testing community

- Look up if there is a testing Meetup[43] in your area. Chances are if there is a testing meetup in your area, they would have listed it on meetup.com (Note: You may be able to attend meetups hosted in other cities if they choose to host their meetup online as well).
- Anything you want to know? Post a question on the Ministry of Testing discussion forum[44]
- Join the Ministry of Testing Slack channel[45]
- Join the TestAutomationU Slack channel[46] (You'll probably benefit from joining this more if you are taking some courses on TestAutomationU).

Better To Be With Developers Than Away From Them

I mean being in the same team compared to being in a separate test team.
I've had much better experiences with developers when "team" refers to a team that has them in it.

Chances are, if you ask any tester who has also worked in both contexts (with developers and away from developers), they'll say the same thing.

Great work and Recognition

It didn't occur to me that great work would not always equal recognition.

[43]https://www.meetup.com/
[44]https://club.ministryoftesting.com/
[45]https://www.ministryoftesting.com/slack_invite
[46]https://tauslacksignupapp.herokuapp.com/

A former manager told me that someone had to see it for it to matter. At work, it seems to me, that the people that climb up the career ladder faster and get recognised, are those that have found a way to draw attention to their successes.

Tip

To be rewarded for good work, people need to see or hear about it.
If you want recognition and reward for the hard work you do, then *someone* has to see it or you need to tell people about it.

You can't just assume that things will work itself out and you'll get the recognition you deserve.

Others' Opinions Of Software Testers Aren't Always a Reflection of You

This mainly applies when you have just started on a software testing project.

Some people think that testers are not technical or they can only write test cases.

Some people think that testers should all be able to write test automation or that testers are inferior to developers.

People I have worked with, have expressed these views to me in the past.

It's taken time for me to realise that it's not personal.

It's a reflection of their past experiences with testers.

Chapter 7: Bug Reports

In chapter one, we looked at this definition[47] of what a bug is:

"Anything that threatens the value of a product"

What is a Bug Report?

> *"A report that outlines information about what is wrong and needs fixing with software or on a website. The report lists reasons, or seen errors, to point out exactly what is viewed as wrong, and also includes a request and/or details for how to address each issue."*

Source: BugHerd[48]

Note: This is the definition of a traditional bug report that is written in a bug tracking tool.

If a bug is found while testing the current user story (and immediately fixed), or part of a different user story (and added to its acceptance criteria), then a written bug report may not be necessary. Instead, you may just communicate this information with a video call or on an instant messaging tool like Slack.

Why You Should Learn How to Write an Effective Bug Report

- So bugs can be prioritised correctly and the team can make

[47] https://www.satisfice.com/blog/archives/572

[48] https://bugherd.com/blog/bug-reporting/

informed decisions about this which bugs to fix before a release (and whether some bugs can wait to be fixed)

- So that developers (and others in your team) don't waste their time investigating bugs because they are unclear or unable to be reproduced
- So there is a record of the behaviour that you have seen, this way if others see the same problem, they can add comments to your bug

Shirin Danehpash, Full Stack Developer at tretton37, shares what has frustrated her in the past, with bug reports she has come across:

> *"When the bug description is not clear, it makes me angry. I cannot start coding and fixing quickly. Also, when the bug is so old and it is not tested after a while to see if it still exists or not. I've spent time trying to recreate a bug but then I realised it was an old bug and the task was not moved to done."*

How to Write an Effective Bug Report

Here is a breakdown of different fields that I have seen in most test management tools used to track bugs, along with information on how to fill in those fields:

Title:

- A brief description of the problem. In some projects, there are naming conventions to the title e.g. an acronym may be at the start dictating the area of the product
- A reader should know what the problem is by just reading the title

- Remember that when people are searching for bugs to see if the one they found has already been raised, they often only look at the title. An unclear title can lead to duplicate bugs being raised.

Description/Summary:

At a bare minimum, I would include the following:

- Actual Result: What did I see/what happened?
- Expected Result: What was I expecting?/ What was supposed to happen?

To strengthen your bug report, I would follow these tips from James Bach's Rapid Software Testing Guide to Bug Reporting[49]*:*

Tip

Write why it's a problem.

Refer to an oracle that explains why the behaviour you see is a problem.

The oracle could be a requirement, a principle or even a person.

Tip

Write why the problem matters.

How can this affect your customers? Why should the people in your team look into *this* bug?

You can also add additional notes on whether you can reproduce the issue consistently, but even if you can't then you should still

[49] https://www.satisfice.com/download/rapid-testing-guide-to-making-good-bug-reports

write the bug report, but it's even more important to note it's an intermittent issue.

Steps to replicate:

- A step by step guide to someone on how to replicate the bug.
- The developer will probably use this to see if they can replicate the bug and investigate it.
- Be specific - use examples if possible. e.g. If there is a specific email address format that should be supported but isn't - write this down.

Other information:

- What investigation have you done to narrow down the issue? Take note of this and include this in your bug report.
- Operating System; Browser; Hardware
- Attach screenshots/videos
- Logs

Shirin Danehpash, on what good bug reports contain, which help her debug and fix bugs:

> *"A good description of the task helps me a lot. If the reporter attaches some screenshots and a short screen video, it is more helpful and efficient.*
>
> *It saves me a lot of time. I can directly start the task instead of going around and asking people about the bug."*

It's not only developers who think along these lines. I asked Anders Jensen, Product Specialist at IKEA, what he has found useful in bug reports:

> *"For bug reports, I prefer a simple model where the reporter always writes the steps taken to encounter the bug, the expected result, the actual result and then adds as much complementary information as possible (screenshots, screen recordings etc.)"*

Common Mistakes

Not mentioning if a bug is intermittent or hard to replicate.
If a bug is intermittent, and then a developer tries to replicate it and can't - don't expect them to keep on trying until they succeed. It's your job to manage their expectations, not their job to just figure it out.

Not attaching screenshots/videos
At the very least attach screenshots.
A picture speaks a thousand words after all.

Not including an expected result
If you point out that the behaviour you are seeing is incorrect, you need to then take the time to investigate and clearly articulate what you are expecting; what should the developer *do* to fix it.

Not including the environment where the bug was found
It's important to include which environment (e.g. Production, System Integration Test) you found the bug in - otherwise, someone may try to reproduce it in the wrong environment and then reject it.

Write "doesn't work"
The number of times I've seen other testers write something along the lines of:

"This ________ doesn't work"

is plain embarrassing.

Instead, write exactly what happens.

Does the page go blank after you click a button?

Does a button flicker or move when you fill in a field?

Be specific.

Chapter 8: Test Cases vs Exploratory Testing vs Ad Hoc Testing

To recap the definitions we initially introduced in Chapter 1:

> *"Exploratory Testing is an approach to software testing that is often described as simultaneous learning, test design and execution.".*
>
> *"Ad hoc testing is random, unstructured testing."*
>
> *"Test cases are a set of preconditions, inputs, actions (where applicable), expected results and postconditions, developed based on test conditions."*

In this chapter, when deciding between test cases, exploratory testing and ad hoc testing, I will focus on explaining why you might choose one over the other and how to go about doing each approach successfully.

When Are Test Cases Most Suitable?

In a regulated industry where you need a lot of written proof of what has been tested
Some industries or scenarios will require it. This doesn't mean you can't do Exploratory Testing at all in these projects, just that you'll need to do at least some Test Cases to prove that the regulations are being met[50].

[50]https://www.atlassian.com/continuous-delivery/software-testing/exploratory-testing

When you need to earn trust in your team, and you lack experience
For a lot of people, testing with test cases is the only "proper" way of doing testing.

If you lack experience (and thus credibility), you may have a hard time convincing your team that you should skip test cases and only do exploratory testing.

Tip

You may need to wait a bit to earn your team's trust and then introduce the idea of exploratory testing once you have proven that you are a good tester.

On one of my first projects (when I had about 1 year of experience at the time), I tried to float the idea of Exploratory Testing past my team soon after I started the project.

It got shut down - no surprises there.

I then focussed on earning my team's trust by doing a great job. I made sure that my test cases and bug reports were well written.

When I tried again in 3-6 months, they were open to trying Exploratory Testing.

For regression testing (if you lack test automation) or smoke testing
For this, I would write high-level test cases (not detailed step by step ones).

A quick way to tell the difference between a high-level test case and a detailed step by step one:

A high-level test case tells you *what* to do; a detailed step by step test case tells you *how* to do it.

Sometimes before a release or when a new feature is added, you may want to use a small set of test cases to check that everything else still looks like it should.

Here are a few examples of what these might look like for an eCommerce platform

High-level test case 1:
Add Product to Favourites list.

High-level test case 2:
(Pre-condition: There are at least 2 products in the Favourites list)
Remove Product from Favourites list.

High-level test case 3:
(Pre-condition: There are at least 2 products in the Favourites list)
Clear/Empty Favourites list

How Do I Write Test Cases?

Pre-conditions:
Here you write what the tester (the person running the test), needs before they start the test.

This can include:

- Access to a certain test environment
- Test Data - e.g. A user with certain characteristics and password for that user

Test Case Steps:
Here is a great example from Guru99 on how Test Case Steps should look like.

Test Case #	Test Case Description	Test Data	Expected Result
1	Check response when valid email and password is entered	Email: guru99@email.com Password: lNf9^Oti7^2h	Login should be successful

To improve this test case, I would add detail to the Expected Result.

What does a successful login look like?

Is there a confirmation message that appears saying "You are now logged in"?

Are you now taken to the User's Profile page?

For further reading on how to write test cases, I suggest you read How to Write Test Cases on Guru99[51].

An Analogy to Explain the Limitation of Test Cases

Both testing and job interviews are information-seeking activities.

- In testing, we are trying to find out information about the Software Under Test.
- In job interviews, the company is trying to seek information on the candidate (actually it goes both ways- the candidate is also trying to seek information on the company as well)

In both instances, you want to make an informed decision.

- In testing, you want to know if the software is ready to go live or proceed to another testing phase (there are other missions related to testing, but sticking to this, for the sake of the analogy).

[51]https://www.guru99.com/test-case.html

- In job interviews, the company wants to know if they want to hire you. (and the candidate wants to know, do I actually want to work here)

Relying solely on test cases is like coming to the job interview with all of your questions pre-planned (on both sides, candidate and company).

This means when you come to the job interview, both sides have a set of questions that they plan to ask and are only seeking the answers to THOSE questions.

There would be no follow-up or investigation based on what the other side said.

Scenario:
Interviewer: Do you have any experience working in an Agile environment? (planned question)
Candidate: Yes, I do. In my previous project, we were working in scrum teams but we didn't have scrum masters.

This answer could be considered strange or would warrant a follow-up. Technically it may "pass" the interviewer's definition of acceptable, but not having a scrum master could be something that warrants investigation and further questioning to see if they were actually working in Scrum teams.

When Is Exploratory Testing The Best Approach?

When you don't have a clear understanding of what expected behaviour is

Unlike test cases that need to pass or fail, with exploratory testing, you can still uncover useful information about the system.

When requirements are changing
Exploratory Testing is often better able to respond to change - writing test cases and then updating them because things change can result in a fair bit of overhead.

When you want fast feedback
Exploratory Testing enables you to get faster feedback about the system, compared to test cases.

How Can I Do Exploratory Testing Effectively?

- Learn how to do Exploratory Testing properly (take a course, read up on it etc.). Don't just try wing it and hope for the best
- Get feedback from others in your team including other testers
- Learn how to communicate your test findings (testing is not just about uncovering information but also about communicating that information)

As a starting point, I suggest you learn how to do Session-Based Test Management as a way to structure your Exploratory Testing.

> *"Session-Based Test Management is a formalized approach that uses the concept of charters and the sessions for performing the Exploratory Testing. A session is not a test case or bug report. It is the reviewable product produced by chartered and uninterrupted test effort. A session can last from 60 to 90 minutes, but there is no hard and fast rule on the time spent for testing.*
>
> *If a session lasts closer to 45 minutes, we call it a short session. If it lasts closer to two hours, we call it a long session. Each session designed depends on the tester and*

> *the charter. After the session is completed, each session is debriefed.*
>
> *The primary objective in the debriefing is to understand and accept the session report. Another objective is to provide feedback and coaching to the tester. The debriefings would help the manager to plan the sessions in future and also to estimate the time required for testing the similar functionality."*

Source: Software Testing Times[52]

Here is a suggested format to structure your testing charters, courtesy of Elisabeth Hendrickson, the author of Explore It!: Reduce Risk and Increase Confidence with Exploratory Testing:

> Explore <registration functionality>
>
> with <unconventional email formats>
>
> to discover <edge cases not covered by form validation>

(Example source: Mirza Sisic's article on Common Misconceptions About Exploratory Testing[53].)

Here is another way you can structure your testing charters, courtesy of Michael D. Kelly's 2012 EuroSTAR presentation[54]:

> My mission is to test <insert risk here> for <insert coverage here>

Some examples he provided using this format:

---

[52]http://softwaretestingtimes.com/2012/04/session-based-test-management-sb.html

[53]https://www.ministryoftesting.com/dojo/lessons/common-misconceptions-about-exploratory-testing

[54]https://www.slideshare.net/EuroSTARConference/mike-kelly-euro-star-webinar

> My mission is to test for SQL injection vulnerabilities for application login and administration screens.
>
> My mission is to test for various boundary errors for Microsoft Word's bullets and numbering feature.

Using Heuristics to do Exploratory Testing Effectively

I'll go into heuristics more in Chapter 9: Testing Against Implicit Requirements, but a great heuristic to get you started with exploratory testing is "San Francisco Depot" or SFDPO.

In his article, James Bach explains[55] what each of these gives product element categories are and the sort of questions you can ask yourself:

Structure (what the product is)

- What files does it have?
- Do I know anything about how it was built?
- Is it one program or many?
- What physical material comes with it?
- Can I test it module by module?

Function (what the product does)

- What are its functions?
- What kind of error handling does it do?
- What kind of user interface does it have?
- Does it do anything that is not visible to the user?
- How does it interface with the operating system?

Data (what it processes)

[55] https://www.stickyminds.com/article/how-do-you-spell-testing

- What kinds of input does it process?
- What does its output look like?
- What kinds of modes or states can it be in?
- Does it come packaged with preset data?
- Is any of its input sensitive to timing or sequencing?

Platform (what it depends upon)

- What operating systems does it run on?
- Does the environment have to be configured in any special way?
- Does it depend on third-party components?

Operations (how it will be used)

- Who will use it?
- Where and how will they use it?
- What will they use it for?
- Are there certain things that users are more likely to do?
- Is there user data we could get to help make the tests more realistic?

When Is Ad Hoc Testing the Best Approach?

For most cases, when someone thinks that Ad Hoc Testing is the best approach - you'll probably be better off doing Exploratory Testing. An exception to this would be bug bashes where you have various people (not just testers) try and find bugs in the application, shortly before you go live.

You may choose to have the people taking part in the Bug Bash, do Ad Hoc Testing, instead of teaching them how to do Exploratory Testing.

Bug Bash

A bug bash is a collaborative event that aims to unearth a large number of bugs within a short timebox. Bug bashes are not an exclusive testers-only event. It can involve developers, testers, product managers, designers, marketers etc.

Source: TestProject[56]

[56] https://blog.testproject.io/2021/04/05/the-ultimate-guide-to-organizing-a-bug-bash/

Chapter 9: Testing Against Implicit Requirements

We have already covered what an implicit requirement is in Chapter 1:

> *"Implicit requirements are features and characteristics of the product experience that customers will expect. In fact, without them, the market would view the product as incomplete.".*

In this chapter, we will focus on how to test against implicit requirements.

Explicit Requirements vs Implicit Requirements

Explicit Requirements	Implicit Requirements
These are explicitly stated either in written documentation or in conversation.	These are not explicitly stated, you need to infer them.
Can come in the form of user stories, acceptance criteria or some other written specifications.	Usually comes from assumed knowledge from someone including the client, business analyst etc.

Why Do You Need to Test Against Implicit Requirements

You need to test against implicit requirements because it is impossible to explicitly state all of the requirements.

I've worked in projects where there was *a lot* of documentation and it seemed that 100% explicit requirements was the goal - but even then there were still gaps that resulted from implicit requirements.

I asked Anders Jensen, Product Specialist at IKEA, if he'd ever been on a project with 100% explicit requirements:

> *"I've never been on a project with 100% explicit requirements but have seen one come close."*

Some level of assumed knowledge is inevitable because it's not worth anyone's time to come up with every single requirement that could possibly arise.

Tip

People often don't realise that they have implicit requirements - so they don't think to communicate them.

It's only later, when they see a working version of the software, that they may realise they had implicit requirements.

They realise that:

We got what we asked for, but not what we were after.

How to Spot Implicit Requirements

Here are some questions to ask yourself when you are going through written requirements, to help you spot implicit requirements:

- Is this *everything* that the Software Under Test (SUT) is expected to do?
- Are negative scenarios referred to in the requirements? If not, how should they be handled?
- What assumptions do we think the person writing the requirements had?
- Are non-functional requirements (e.g. Security, Accessibility, Performance) explicitly referred to? (These are often expected but people don't always think to write them down)
- Are there any laws or local regulations that are assumed to be covered?

Anders Jensen shares his thoughts on implicit requirements and his expectations when writing user stories:

> *"I think that a user story in itself is written to facilitate discussions and therefore always has some implicit parts to it."*

What Shapes Implicit Requirements

This generally falls into two categories:

1. People's past experiences
2. What people assume to be a given

People's past experiences

The level of requirements on projects people have worked on often determines what "enough" looks like.
If someone has only worked on projects with a lot of detailed, written requirements, then they are likely to provide a similar level (or at least try to) on your project.

Past projects and past personal experiences
It's not just the level of requirements (in previous projects) that will shape implicit requirements but also the past work and personal experiences of your colleagues.

What people assume to be a given

In the past, this is what I have seen people often assume to be a given:

A certain level of performance
A few seconds to submit a form is one thing.

One minute is another.

Even if you didn't have explicit performance requirements on your project, customers will almost definitely complain if it takes them too long to use your product.

Here I will share a story where I didn't test against an implicit performance requirement and what happened as a result:

> Near the start of my career I was on a project that was building an inventory count feature. Our go-live date was shortly before the annual stocktake season, where a lot of retailers count all of their products.
>
> I had tested against the user stories, paired with other testers and I honestly thought I did a great job testing the feature.

> How wrong I was.
>
> There was an implicit requirement that the feature would support thousands (even tens of thousands) of products. But I had only tested it with up until about a hundred products.
>
> Our release did not go well. Our team had to spend time in the evenings because we missed this implicit requirement.

User Feedback

People want to know if what they have done is successful or not. They also want to know that they are waiting for a screen to load by seeing a loading icon (especially if something is taking more than a second to load)

People don't want to wait 10 seconds, while looking at a blank screen.

Jakob Nielsen's first Usability Heuristic for User Interface Design[57] applies here:

1. Visibility of system status

> *"The design should always keep users informed about what is going on, through appropriate feedback within a reasonable amount of time.*
>
> *When users know the current system status, they learn the outcome of their prior interactions and determine next steps. Predictable interactions create trust in the product as well as the brand."*

While this implicit requirement does fall into design, I do think it's helpful for testers to have a basic understanding of good design practices to be able to perform their role effectively.

---

[57]https://www.nngroup.com/articles/ten-usability-heuristics/

Security
Things like passwords displaying as dots or asterisks are often a given.

Also, that secure information is encrypted when it's been sent.

Browser and device support
Even if you don't have explicit requirements for browser and device support - there is still definitely a level of expected support.

A useful site regarding browser and device usage, per country, is Statcounter Global Stats.[58]

I once had to test a feature for a company that was added to the Chinese market. You'll notice in the graph below that there are a few browsers in China, that are not available in either my home country, New Zealand, nor where I live, Sweden.

According to this graph, UC Browser was the second most used Browser from November 2020 to November 2021.

Meanwhile, 360 Safe Browser and QQ Browser each had over 5%.

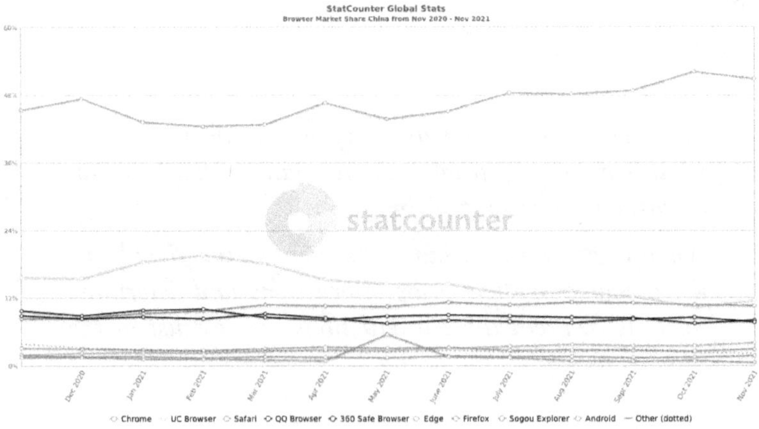

When I was asked to help test this feature, nobody told me about these browsers, and I didn't think to ask.

[58]https://gs.statcounter.com/browser-market-share

I only happened to stumble across this because I saw some users in China raise other bugs for a different feature against one of these (previously unknown to me) browsers.

Backwards compatibility
Depending on the project, some products would require more backwards compatibility than others.

A mobile app game targeted at young kids may require you to have quite a bit of backwards compatibility since one may assume that parents give their children their older devices to play with.

Meanwhile, an app that people need to use for work may not require as much backwards compatibility since users are more likely to have access to software updates and newer devices.

Heuristics and Oracles You Can Use to Help You Test Against Implicit Requirements

FEW HICCUPPS.

I first came across this in the BBST Foundations Course in 2013, and I have come back to this throughout my software testing career.

It stands for:[59]

Familiarity
Explainability
World

History
Image
Comparable Products
Claims

[59]https://www.developsense.com/blog/2012/07/few-hiccupps/

User Desires
Product Itself
Purpose
Statutes

These are consistency heuristics, that we test to make sure that each aspect is consistent with the bullet point.

I'll elaborate on each one in detail, below.

Thanks to Michael Bolton for providing these definitions in his blog post[60]

Familiarity
Inconsistency with Familiarity
We expect the system to be *inconsistent* with patterns of familiar problems.

By using this heuristic, you don't fall into traps where you are only looking for familiar kinds of bugs.

> *"Focusing on familiar problems might divert our attention away from other consistency principles that are more relevant to the task at hand. Perhaps most importantly, a premature search for bugs might distract us from a crucial task in the early stages of testing: a search for benefits and features that will help us to develop better ideas about value, risk, and coverage, and will inform deeper and more thoughtful testing."*

For example: A familiar problem I often see is lack of useful information to help people fill in certain fields (no tooltips or helpful error messages) - if you were testing an internal-facing system, this problem may be considered less significant than if you were testing a system that faced the general public. This is because presumably, you can run workshops and train up users at your company. Also,

[60]https://www.developsense.com/blog/2012/07/few-hiccupps/

you may assume that users at your company would be more patient than the general public.

Explainability
We expect a system to be understandable to the degree that we can articulately explain its behaviour to ourselves and others.

For example: Let's say you worked on an eCommerce website, and the new feature you added is emailing someone (or yourself) a list of what's in your Shopping Cart. That should be pretty easy to explain.

World
We expect the product to be consistent with things that we know about or can observe in the world.

For example: In a past project, I saw that they only accepted addresses entered as STREET NUMBER then STREET NAME, but I knew there are a lot of countries that have STREET NAME then STREET NUMBER. The system was supposed to be used by users all over the world.

History
We expect the present version of the system to be consistent with past versions of it.

For example: Is there a specific menu and sub-menu structure that users might be expecting? (Based on their use of previous versions of your system)

Image
We expect the system to be consistent with an image that the organization wants to project, with its brand, or with its reputation.

For example: A payments app presumably wants to give the image that your money is secure with them and that they are trustworthy - a lot of typos might not give a user that impression.

Comparable Products
We expect the system to be consistent with systems that are in some way comparable.

For example: If other spreadsheet apps support conditional formatting, any new spreadsheet apps should support conditional formatting.

Claims
We expect the system to be consistent with things important people say about it.

For example: If a payment app claims you can transfer money to a friend automatically, that your friend can see the money in their account almost instantaneously.

User Desires
We believe that the system should be consistent with ideas about what reasonable users might want.

For example: If you are applying for a pre-approved bank loan application with your bank, then any information your bank already has on you, would be pre-filled in the application to save you time.

(the) Product itself
We expect each element of the system (or product) to be consistent with comparable elements in the same system.

For example: That all email fields have the same validation on a website

Purpose
We expect the system to be consistent with the explicit and implicit uses to which people might put it.

For example: That you are able to send and receive messages using a messaging app.

Statutes
We expect a system to be consistent with laws or regulations that are relevant to the product or its use.

For example: That websites in Europe are compliant with GDPR.

RCRCRC - A Heuristic for Regression Testing

Karen N. Johnson, Director of Engineering Effectiveness at Grainger, came up with a very useful heuristic for Regression Testing.

It stands for:[61]
Recent
Core
Risk
Configuration sensitive
Repaired
Chronic

Below is verbatim from her post:

Recent
New features, new areas of code are more vulnerable

Core
Essential functions must continue to work

Risk
Some areas of an application pose more risk

Configuration sensitive
Code that's dependent on environment settings can be vulnerable

Repaired
Bug fixes can introduce new issues

Chronic
Some areas in an application may be perpetually sensitive to breaking

---

[61] http://karennicolejohnson.com/2009/11/a-heuristic-for-regression-testing/

Chapter 10: Test Automation

As someone who doesn't have a technical background, I had put test automation on a pedestal for the first few years of my career. I remember it was very intimidating.

But it needn't be.

When you break it down and find the right resources - learning (and applying) test automation can be very approachable.

What is Test Automation?

According to Testim:[62]

> *"Test automation is the practice of running tests automatically, managing test data, and utilizing results to improve software quality. It's primarily a quality assurance measure, but its activities involve the commitment of the entire software production team. From business analysts to developers and DevOps engineers, getting the most out of test automation takes the inclusion of everyone."*

Test automation isn't limited to this.

Sebastian Holgersson, Senior Consultant at an IT consultancy, pointed out that:

---

[62]https://www.testim.io/blog/what-is-test-automation/

> *"Test automation (to me) is often about improving tooling. Have computers do a lot of the boring and repetitive stuff, so that you can spend more time on the interesting parts.*
>
> *For example: Being able to quickly and automatically instantiate an environment can be part of test automation, even if it doesn't mean that the tests themselves are automated.*
>
> *Another example might be to create a tool that takes screenshots of all the various parts of a page, so that a human can quickly have a look and make sure that things don't look completely bad.*
>
> *A test doesn't have to be 100% automated, it's often good enough to automate the parts that make sense to automate."*

Why Should You Learn Test Automation?

Kim Engel answers this question, in her blog post, 'As a software tester, do I need to learn about automation?'[63] using the analogy of learning how to drive a car.

> *"Let's step back for a minute and put this another way, "Do I need to learn how to drive a car?.*
>
> *Well you could walk, or take the bus, or pay a taxiUber driver to drive you around. These are all valid choices. But there's a big advantage in being able to drive, for times when driving is the best option.*

[63]https://isitgoodenoughyet.com/2016/07/24/as-a-software-tester-do-i-need-to-learn-about-automation/

> *So my answer is no, you don't need to learn automation skills, but having those skills will let you make informed decisions about the most efficient way to approach each testing task, with a wider range of options available to you."*

Another key benefit of learning how to write automation is that it improves your technical understanding of how software is built.

To implement effective test automation, you (often) need to be able to:

- Understand which classes handle which features
- How/if features are dependant on each other
- Read code and understand what it's doing and what method(s) are being called

Sebastian Holgersson shares his experience on when he was a consultant manager at an IT consultancy:

> *"I'd suggest that testers play around with test automation even if they have no intention of actually working with it. It's hard to understand when those tools could be useful and what their limitations are if you haven't used them before.*
>
> *If you as a tester don't know anything about test automation, it's hard to push back when a manager is inspired by a talk at a conference and suggests that everything should be automated, without necessarily understanding the matter fully."*

When Should You Write Test Automation?

Tip

Just because you can write test automation, doesn't mean you should.

There are times in which writing test automation is not the best investment of your time or your team's time.

Here are some questions to ask yourself when considering whether to write test automation:

- Are there looking to be a lot of changes in the area I plan to write tests in?
- Is this a long-running project and will there be someone to maintain the test automation suite, or at least keep track of results, once I am done with it? (This applies if you are a consultant and will need to hand it over)
- Is this the best use of my time? Remember: Often, you don't reap the benefits of test automation until later, when it's actually running.
- Is there any manual intervention needed for this test? (If some sort of visual confirmation or 2 Factor Authentication is needed in the test, you may struggle to justify writing test automation for these cases)
- Is the intended user of the system a machine or a person?

To elaborate, Sebastian Holgerssson points out that:

> *"If you're testing an API, you're testing the ability for a computer to speak to this computer. Test automation is likely to be useful here.*

If you're testing a video game, you're partially testing whether this is a fun experience for a human - this is not something that should be automated.

A frontend application, where users are expected to navigate using touch screen/mouse+keyboard interfaces can only be partially tested using automation. As a tester, you also want to be able to test whether the UX makes sense etc, which automation will never let you do."

How Do You Gain Test Automation Skills?

Taking the first step is the hardest. It can seem intimidating for someone to gain test automation skills, especially if you don't come from a technical/coding background.

You have a few options in gaining test automation skills, let's look at each of them in turn.

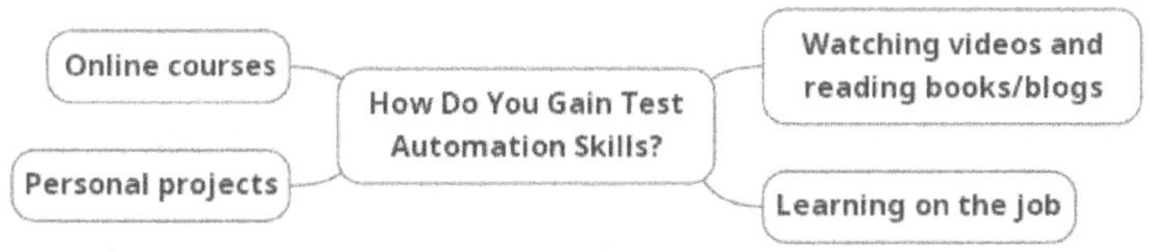

1. Watching videos and reading books/blogs
There are a lot of videos you can watch online that will show you how to write test automation.
There are also numerous books and blogs which attempt to teach beginners how to get started with test automation.
However, I advise against this approach being the main way of

learning test automation. But feel free to use this as a supplement to one of the other options.

The problem with only watching videos or reading about test automation is that to learn how to write test automation - nothing beats actually doing it. You need to write code.

Another potential problem with only watching videos is that, as a beginner, it can be hard to gauge whether the person has a solid understanding of test automation. If you lack the context of what's happening, then it can be hard to learn something useful from a short technical video.

However, watching videos and reading about test automation can help you learn about some theoretical concepts or how to tackle specific problems, so there is still definitely some value in this.

2. Online courses
Compared with watching videos, courses often provide you with context, so you know why you're doing what you're doing.

With online courses, you can watch and listen to someone explain different concepts related to test automation and how they approach it.

More importantly, online courses tend to offer some sort of structure.

The best online courses will be structured in such a way that they enable you to build on what you already know. If you don't have any prior coding knowledge, then there are plenty of options out there that will cater to this.

Lastly, some online courses provide hands-on activities where you can solve a different problem using the skills and techniques they have taught you in previous exercises.

This course on Test Automation University provides activities that allow you to apply what you have learned.

- Selenium Webdriver with Java[64]

3. Learning on the job
The key benefit of this approach is that you will be able to apply what you have learned and you will learn the programming language and test automation framework that is needed.

In the past, I have learned various programming languages and test automation frameworks in my spare time to upskill.

The problem was that I often forgot a lot of what I learned if I never had an opportunity to apply what I learned. (As previously mentioned, a well structured online course can address this, if it has activities where you have the chance to apply what you learned).

Learning on the job also helps with motivation. It's easier to be motivated to learn, when you know that you'll get to apply it.

Aside from the key benefit of being able to apply your knowledge, you'll also be able to ask your colleagues questions and learn from them.

You can pair up with your colleagues as they write test automation.

They can set up tasks for you to do, to help you familiarise yourself with the test automation setup.

You can ask them why they do things the way they do, and for any tips for future test automation projects.

4. Personal projects
You can create your own personal projects and write test automation frameworks for existing websites and apps.

Here are a few websites you can use for practice to get you started:

- http://the-internet.herokuapp.com/
- http://automationpractice.com/index.php
- https://restful-booker.herokuapp.com/

[64]https://testautomationu.applitools.com/selenium-webdriver-tutorial-java/

The Recommended Reading section has more practice websites and apps you can use to practice your test automation skills on.

You can create repos in either GitHub or GitLab.

Which Programming Language and Test Automation Framework Should You Learn?

What programming language is your team currently using?

Tip

If you are already on a project, then learn the programming language that the developers on your project use, and a test automation framework that is suitable for it.

For example: If you are on a web-based project where the front-end is written in Javascript, I suggest you learn Cypress. Cypress would be a great starting point because it's a Javascript End to End Testing Framework, so developers can also contribute, there is also plenty of online resources to help you learn this.

A lot of the knowledge you gain by learning a programming language and test automation framework can carry over to other domains as well. If you learn how to test a REST API in Java, then doing so later in Python or Javascript isn't such a big jump. Since you know how the framework works, then you just need to adjust to the new language.

If you aren't on a project, yet, then you have a few options.

> *"Analysis paralysis is way worse than taking a risk and failing, which is actually learning."* - Indie Hackers

To avoid this, where you spend too much time researching what you should learn (and no time actually learning test automation), I will make 3 suggestions:

1. Selenium Webdriver in Java
2. Cypress in Javascript
3. API Testing in Python

Test Automation University offers great courses for all of the above.

Remember: Don't get too attached to one tool or overthink the decision on what you should learn first.

How good is the documentation and available online resources?
It's a lot easier to learn something when you have good resources.

I suggest you lean towards a programming language and test automation framework that has plenty of online resources that you can turn to as you learn.

How Do I Find the Time to Gain Test Automation Skills?

This is easy if you get to learn on the job, as you don't have to use up your personal time.

If you need to upskill on your own time I suggest you keep the following in mind:

1. Set monthly goals, and break this down into weeks and even days (if you are looking to put in a little bit of time each day)

2. Remember: Consistency is key. It's easy to lose motivation after a few days or long evenings upskilling
3. If this is important to you, you need to prioritise this over things like social media and other websites that eat into your time. I would timebox any time spent on "time-waster" sites or avoid these sites altogether.
4. If you find that you don't want to learn how to use a tool, then reconsider whether you are using the right resources to learn it or whether you should be learning to use that tool in the first place. If you are learning how to use a tool, it should make you feel like you are solving a problem - it shouldn't feel painful.
5. A key factor in learning test automation is to have an interest in it. You may need to find a way to *become* interested in it. If you try to learn test automation, even though you hate it, it just means you're learning to do a job that you may never like.

Mnemonic for creating valuable test automation.

Here are two mnemonics that can help a tester create valuable test automation.

Let's start with TRIMS[65], created by Richard Bradshaw, CEO of Ministry of Testing and Mark Winteringham, COO of Ministry of Testing.

Targeted

There are two things to focus on here: risk and implementation.

According to Richard Bradshaw:

[65]https://automationintesting.com/2019/08/trims-automation-in-testing-strategy

> *"We need to be selective with what we automate because we can't automate everything. I've seen folk try, they believe they get close but then enter the very difficult to break the cycle of break-fix-break-fix. They believe all the checks are equal and have to fix them all. To break that circle they need to look at what risk each check is mitigating and delete the ones of little value."*

With regards to implementation, you need to look at where you should implement the automated check; at which layer or seam.

Testability is key here. While you may identify the lowest layer at which you can mitigate the risk (e.g. the API layer), if testability doesn't support it, then you need to have your automated checks on the UI level instead.

Reliable

Automated checks should bring your attention to genuine change you need to investigate - not false positives because your tests are flaky.

Informative

Automated checks detect change. Automated checks need to provide information to enable you to investigate that change and determine whether or not there is a problem.

Good naming conventions of your tests and methods are helpful here.

- Example of a good naming convention:

testLoginWrongPassword
(Here we know what our test is focussing on)

- Example of a poor naming convention:

testLoginError
(What error? Could be any error)

Maintainable

To ensure your test automation is maintainable you need to take advantage of design patterns and good coding practices.

Examples of design patterns:
1. Screenplay pattern
According to SerenityJS[66]:

> *"Instead of focusing on low-level, interface-centric interactions, you describe your test scenarios in a similar way you'd describe them to a human being - an actor in Screenplay-speak. You write simple, readable and highly-reusable code that instructs the actors what activities to perform and what things to check. The domain-specific test language you create is used to express screenplays - the activities for the actors to perform in a given test scenario."*

2. The Page Object Model (commonly referred to as POM)

According to the Selenium website:[67]

> *"A page object is an object-oriented class that serves as an interface to a page of your AUT. The tests then use the methods of this page object class whenever they need to interact with the UI of that page."*

[66]https://serenity-js.org/handbook/design/screenplay-pattern.html
[67]https://www.selenium.dev/documentation/guidelines/page_object_models/

Examples of good coding practices:

- Making sure your code is readable
- Writing comments to ensure your code is understandable

Speedy

Here you are encouraged to focus on rapid execution and maintenance - within the constraints of your system's testability.

However, remember that faster doesn't always mean better - you don't want speed to come at the cost of reliability or informativeness.

Now let's look at SACRED[68], a mnemonic created by Richard Bradshaw. (The mnemonic below is copied from his post almost verbatim)

State Management

This is all about managing the state of the application. This includes deploying the system, configuring it, setting feature flags and of course test data setup.

Actions

The actions you need to take to trigger the specific behaviour of the system. This could be clicking around a UI, filling in fields or waiting for elements. Or, this could be calling APIs with specific data in a specific order.

[68] https://thefriendlytester.co.uk/2019/06/new-whiteboard-testing-video-sacred

Codified Oracle

Oracles are what we used to determine if the behaviour we are seeing is desired or not. In an automated check, we tend to codify one of two of them, known as assertions. They are really important to get right, to maximise the value we get from our checks.

Reporting

The reporting takes on two forms in SACRED. The first is for reporting the results of your checks. Do you need to hook into your CI (Continuous Integration) server, a test management tool or something like Slack? The second side of reporting is getting your automated check to report as much as possible about failures to you. Such as log files, screenshots and decent error messages.

Execution

Where are your checks going to be executed? Have you designed them to work there? We often focus on getting them working on our local machine and overlook where they will finally be executed.

Deterministic

Automated checks need to be deterministic, they should do exactly the same thing over and over again.

Chapter 11: How To Prevent Bugs

It's not hard to find articles online saying that the sooner you find a bug, the cheaper it is to fix.

You might also see graphs that look something like this (which, to be honest, is an oversimplification of real-life).

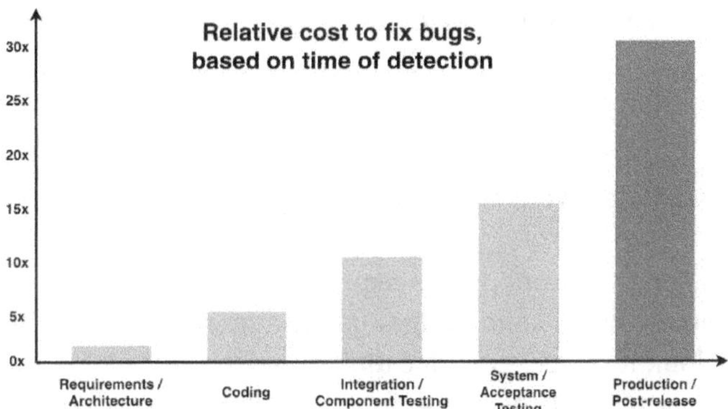

Source: DeepSource[69]

However, I've found there isn't a whole lot of information out there on exactly how to prevent bugs in the early stages of a software development project. i.e. before code is written, in the first bar of this graph.

Here I would like to share exactly how I have helped prevent bugs on projects and how I have helped others come up with ideas on how to prevent bugs as well.

[69]https://deepsource.io/blog/exponential-cost-of-fixing-bugs/

Make Sure The Requirements Are Testable

We'll dive deeper into testability in the next chapter, but it's important to be aware of testability of requirements when it comes to preventing bugs.

According to Ranorex[70]:

> *"A testable requirement describes a single function or behavior of an application in a way that makes it possible to develop tests to determine whether the requirement has been met.*
>
> *To be testable, a requirement must be clear, measurable, and complete, without any ambiguity."*

Here is what you want to avoid:

- Subjective or ambiguous requirements
- Requirements containing implementation details (i.e. button colour, text size, exact location on screen etc.)
- Covering more that one function; ideally each requirement should be able to be built and tested by itself

Below is an example of Ranorex[71], of how a requirement that needs to be broken down, looks like:

> *"When at least one matching item is found, display up to 20 matching inventory items, in a grid or list and using the sort order according to the user preference settings."*

And once it's broken down, it becomes 3 separate requirements:

---

[70] https://www.ranorex.com/blog/10-best-practices-8-write-testable-requirements/
[71] https://www.ranorex.com/blog/10-best-practices-8-write-testable-requirements/

> *"When at least one matching item is found, display up to 20 matching inventory items."*
>
> *"Display search results in a grid or list according to the user preference settings."*
>
> *"Display search results in the sort order according to the user preference settings."*

Make Sure The Frontend And Backend Are Compatible

What do I mean by "Frontend"?

This is what the user interacts with; it is what you see on a computer or mobile screen.

What do I mean by "Backend"?

This is what happens "behind the scenes".

According to Concepta[72]:

> *"The term "front-end" refers to the user interface, while "back-end" means the server, application and database that work behind the scenes to deliver information to the user.*
>
> *The user enters a request through the interface.*
>
> *It's then verified and communicated to the server, which pulls the necessary data from the database and sends it back to the user."*

[72]https://www.conceptatech.com/blog/difference-front-end-back-end-development

Are they compatible with each other?

It's important to have both frontend and backend validation.

It's also important to make sure that your frontend and backend (validation) are compatible.

If you get access to the API/backend documentation and the UI designs, you can compare the two and communicate your planned testing with your team.

Make sure that your frontend validation is the same as or stricter than your backend validation.

You don't want your frontend to let in input that your backend will later reject.

For example:
In the designs you see that a user has to fill in a profile form with the following information:

- First name (mandatory)
- Last name
- Phone number (mandatory)

You see in the API documentation the following:

- First name (mandatory)
- Last name (mandatory)
- Phone number (mandatory)

There will be a problem.

The backend requires the last name but the front end doesn't enforce this.

Here are some things to watch out for.

- Mandatory Fields (including conditionally mandatory)
- Input type (alphanumeric)
- Input Length (i.e. number of characters; min, max)

What is a conditionally mandatory field?

A conditionally mandatory field is a field that becomes mandatory based on the input of another.

For example: If you click on the "Overseas" radio button, for a postage app, then the country field may become mandatory in the address section.

How To Have A Testing Discussion

A testing discussion is a team discussion on exactly how a feature will be tested. The goals are to clear up any misunderstandings and unearth any preventable issues.

I've found testing discussions to be one of the most valuable things in helping prevent bugs. In these discussions, your team has a great opportunity to bounce ideas off each other, raise concerns and most importantly, clear up misunderstandings.

I have found these are easiest to have when the designs are done or at least once you have a draft of the designs you can use to base your discussions around.

When should I have a testing discussion?

You can choose to have it at refinement, so it's not yet another meeting for the team to attend.

Or you can have it as a separate meeting, where it's the sole focus.

It's up to you to determine what would suit your team best.

Prepare for a testing discussion.

Note: I tend to go with testing notes, instead of test cases - but ultimately it's up to you to decide on what's best for your project and realistically, what you can do a walkthrough with.

Before you hold the testing discussion, you need to prepare.

- Go through the designs and any documentation you have
- Note down anything you are unsure about including questions
- Explicitly write down any assumptions you have
- Write down how you would test different scenarios including negative scenarios

Here is an example of how my testing notes would look like if I were to test a feedback form[73]: (I would probably go into more detail in real life, but this will serve well to demonstrate how testing notes should look like)

In this example, I have access to this design, but no access to the API documentation.

[73]http://zero.webappsecurity.com/feedback.html

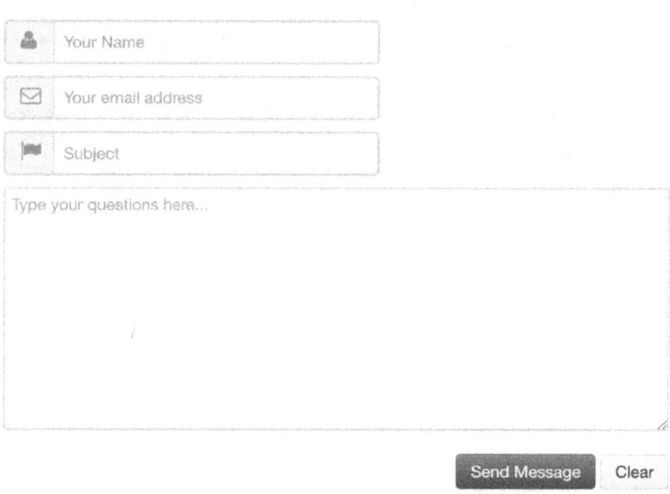

Feedback

Our Frequently Asked Questions area will help you with many of your inquiries.
If you can't find your question, return to this page and use the e-mail form below.

IMPORTANT! This feedback facility is not secure. Please do not send any account information in a message sent from here.

Your Name

Your email address

Subject

Type your questions here...

Send Message
Clear

Assumptions:

- All of the fields are mandatory
- Send Message button is disabled until all of the fields have valid data
- We can submit this form in all of our website's currently-supported browsers (I will assume here that this has already been agreed upon)
- As soon as I start filling in the fields, the grey placeholder text will be replaced by the text I type in.
- Email address must be in XX@XX.XX format

- A confirmation message will appear after I submit valid data
- An email confirmation will be sent to the email entered into the email address field

Questions

- What is the purpose of the feedback form? What problem are we trying to solve by implementing it?
- What is the maximum number of characters allowed in each field?
- Are there any characters on a deny-list in each field? (I suggest you have an allow-list instead)
- What error codes do we need to be aware of?

How I would test:
(This isn't an exhaustive list, but merely a starting point to provide an example.)

- Test with the following input and submit on the latest versions of Chrome, Safari, Firefox and Edge. (Name: Nicola, Email: test@example.com, Subject: Test subject, Questions: here is a question)
- Enter input into all of the fields then click on 'Clear', expect that all of the fields are cleared.
- Enter input into 2 of the fields then click on 'Clear', expect that those 2 fields are cleared.
- Keep entering input into each field and take note of the max limit each field allows

Note: It's important to be clear in our testing notes, don't worry about being wrong. The clearer your testing notes, the better discussions your team can have - which will help your team prevent bugs.

Here is a step-by-step guide to holding a testing discussion:

1. **Book it in**

Once you have a design/set of designs to base your discussion around, for a new feature, book the testing discussion in the calendar. Ideally, you want to do this soon enough so that developers haven't started coding yet. (If you've ever heard of "Shift Left" in testing, this is one example of this.)

Invite anyone who has been involved with the feature or will be involved with the feature.

2. **Set the expectations**

At the start of the meeting, set the expectations.
Here is what I tell everyone:

> *I wanted to take the opportunity to go over this feature and make sure I understand everything correctly for when we test it.*
>
> *If I have misunderstood how anything should work, please correct me.*
>
> *I want to hear your ideas on how best to test this, there's probably something I'm missing.*

I'm being clear that I am open to feedback, but more importantly, that I am open to being corrected and that I probably missed something.

3. **Go through the questions and assumptions**

I would have sent out these notes to everyone about an hour before the meeting.

I tend to start with going through the questions and assumptions I made.

As we answer the questions I have, I write down the answers. I also take notes on if any of my assumptions turned out to be wrong.

I then ask if anyone else has any questions.

I also write down these questions and their answers.

Here is how the conversation might look like:

> Me: I'm not seeing any red asterisks in the designs, so I'm assuming all of the fields are mandatory?
>
> Designer: The subject field isn't needed.
>
> Me: Ok, can we add some visual cue to the mandatory fields then?
>
> Backend developer: Actually I need the subject field to have input.
>
> Designer: Ok we'll make sure we have the subject field then. I'll just make some updates to the designs and add red asterisks to all of the fields there (since that's what we have for other mandatory fields elsewhere on our website).

4. **Go through how I would test it**
Similar to before, ask if there is anything I am missing.

Ask if there is anything else I should test.

5. **Double check, is there anything else?**
Before closing the meeting, I ask everyone is there anything else that is unclear about this feature and how this will be or should be tested?

I also say, if you think of anything just let me know.

Sometimes, people need time to process information.

6. **Thank everyone for their time, send out notes**
At the end of the meeting, I thank everyone for their time and say I'll send an updated version of the testing notes (based on new information uncovered at the meeting) to everyone.

7. **After the meeting**
I email everyone the updated notes and I update any relevant documentation that could be affected.

The reason I send out the updated notes is to make sure we have a shared understanding of what was discussed and what was agreed upon.

Tip

You might need some time to get used to holding testing discussions but over time you will get better at it. Your team will also learn to appreciate the information these discussions uncover.

Applying Heuristics To Bug Prevention

You can apply the heuristics you learned in Chapters 8 and 9, to bug prevention. Feel free to go back over these chapters for ideas.

Some of my favourites that I find to be particularly useful at this stage include:

- Michael Bolton's Consistency Within Product Heuristic
- Jakob Nielsen's first Usability Heuristic for User Interface Design
- James Bach's SFDPO Data Heuristic
- Michael Bolton's Explainability Heuristic

If you are overwhelmed as to where to start, when it comes to preventing bugs, these heuristics are a great starting point.

Additional Things To Be Aware Of

- Are there any dependencies within the app we need to be aware of?
- Are there any external dependencies (e.g. 3rd party ones) that we need to be aware of?
- Examples are a great way to make sure everyone is on the same page; they help make concepts more concrete for people (I use examples *a lot* when I am discussing how I would test something).

Chapter 12: Ask For Testability

To recap, Testability is:

> *"Testability is about how easy it is to test something. How easy it is to retrieve the information we need."*

Expectations Around Testability

At the start of my career, I didn't know what "Testability" was. In fact, I had never heard of it.

When I was faced with something new to test, I would ask myself:

> *How do I test this, given the limitations I face?*

These limitations could be in the form of:

- lack of test data (as I might not have access to create test data)
- unstable test environments
- no access to logs etc.

I honestly thought this was pretty normal - so I didn't question it.

Over time, I realised it wasn't a question of whether or not it's normal **but whether or not something can be done about it**.

These days, when I am faced with something new to test, I ask myself:

- What do I want to test?
- What can be improved/changed so that I can test what I want to test?

The key part here is that my expectations changed.

Now I know that testability is something you can ask for (or do something about).

How You Can Ask For Testability

If you are struggling with covering some scenarios or writing some tests, because of your current setup, I suggest you talk to the developers in your team to see what your options are.

I suggest the following format:

- This is what I would like to test
- This is the risk I am covering with this test/these tests
- What can be done to make this happen?
- What do you need from me, to help make this happen?

Some Examples

Automatibility

Put simply, automatibility is how easy it is to test an application with test automation.

I've come across applications that were pretty easy to set up and write test automation for and others that were very frustrating.

Here are a few examples of problems I have faced around automatibility and the solutions

1. *Problem: No good selectors for me to interact with*
Solution: Ask the developers to add IDs

2. *Problem: Unable to get past a 2FA screen*
Solutions discussed:

- Hardcode the 2FA 4 digit pincode
- Skip 2FA screen altogether in the test environment

A key thing to consider when it comes to automatiblity is tool selection.

If you decide to write your user interface in some proprietary system like Unity or something similar, it might be a lot more difficult to utilise test automation.

If you create your user interface in something like React, it'll be a lot easier to utilise test automation on this. There would be a lot of resources and tools available.

Controllability

According to Wikipedia:

> *"The degree to which it is possible to control the state of the component under test (CUT) as required for testing."*

In a past project, I had to deal with timeouts for slow test environments. I asked the developers to adjust the timeouts in the test environments because our test environment was too slow.

In Production, we wanted an error to appear after 5 seconds, but in our test environments, it took 30 seconds for transactions to load. This meant errors would always appear.

Therefore, we changed the amount of time a user needs to wait for an error to appear from 5 seconds to 60 seconds.

A great tool that helps with controllability is Charles Proxy.[74]

According to their site:

> *"Charles is an HTTP proxy / HTTP monitor / Reverse Proxy that enables a developer to view all of the HTTP and SSL / HTTPS traffic between their machine and the Internet. This includes requests, responses and the HTTP headers (which contain the cookies and caching information)."*

By using breakpoints in Charles, you can control the network requests and responses for the app you are testing.

You can trigger errors manually. For example, instead of always getting a 200 OK Response Code, you can see what the screen should display if there is an Internal Server Error (500 Response Code).

I have written a Testing With Charles Proxy blog series[75] that can help you get started.

Observability

Observability concerns your ability to see what's happening.

To know what's actually happening, you shouldn't just be looking at the UI.

The UI is what's displayed to the user - it doesn't tell the full story.

I'd like to share a story on the consequences of a lack of observability.

---

[74]https://www.charlesproxy.com/

[75]https://nicolalindgren.com/2022/01/17/testing-with-charles-proxy-part-1/

> In one of my first projects, we had to test on Internet Explorer (it was an internal-facing application and Internet Explorer was the only supported browser). As far as our team knew, there was no good way to view network traffic.
>
> We had to create user profiles, then later search for them and edit them. After "successfully" creating a user profile, a confirmation message would display on the screen.
>
> However, we later found that the user profiles were never created in the first place.
>
> Poof.
>
> Gone.
>
> This was a very frustrating environment to test in. I remember often questioning myself as I tested, before writing more detailed notes to keep track of the user profiles I allegedly created.

These days we have in-built browser tools like Chrome Developer Tools - which would have aided in the lack of observability in my story.

In most projects, you can also ask for access to the logs.

What is a log?

"A log is the automatically produced and time-stamped documentation of events relevant to a particular system."

According to Matt Heuser, in his article in TechTarget[76]:

---

[76]https://www.techtarget.com/searchapparchitecture/tip/5-key-software-testability-characteristics

> *"Effective system logs tell you what happened and when. For high software testability, set up logs so that you can list every web service call and see who made it, when they made it and in which order it was processed.*
>
> *These logs should also be searchable and provide explanations for why an end-user saw an error, even if that error doesn't appear in subsequent requests."*

Chances are, the developers in your team are using logs to debug any problems they might come across.

If you are struggling to understand what the logs are saying, or how to navigate through the logs - talk to your team about it and someone should (hopefully) help you.

Tip

Make sure the logs are accessible (easy to get to) and consumable (able to be read).

Examples of log frameworks include:

- Winston
- Log4j
- Splunk Log Observer
- SumoLogic
- Lograge

Monitoring tools can also help with observability. Monitoring the application lets you leverage the issues your customers see when you're trying to reproduce bugs. You can also get inspiration for tests.

Some examples provided by Sebastian Holgersson:

- Prometheseus (Gives you the answers to questions like "What endpoints are seeing the most 500 errors?", "Which browsers are the most popular?" etc. These can be useful for tracking down bugs in production and for creating realistic test cases)
- Sentry[77] (A key benefit here is that you can see what error(s) your customers are experiencing)
- Kibana[78] (Similar to Splunk, helps you search logs.)
- Grafana[79] (Here you can create dashboards.)

Using Rob Meaney's 10 P's of Testability

Based on Rob Meaney's 10 P's of Testability[80], here are some more ways in which you can ask for (and thus advocate for) more testability:

- PROJECT: Is the team provided with enough time, resources and autonomy to do great testing?
- PIPELINE: Does your deployment pipeline set up enable fast, reliable, accessible, comprehensive feedback on what happens in production? If not, how can we make this happen?
- PRODUCT: Is the product understandable so that we can test it? (i.e.Do we know what the product is supposed to do?)

Remember

A lack of testability isn't something you need to accept. There are steps you can take to improve it.

[77] https://sentry.io/welcome/
[78] https://www.elastic.co/kibana/
[79] https://grafana.com/
[80] https://teatimewithtesters.com/untangling-testability/

A lack of testability isn't a problem for testers, it's a problem for testing. And therefore a problem for the team.

Chapter 13: Preparing For Releases

While there is a lot a team can do to be confident with their releases, this chapter will focus primarily on what individual testers can do to contribute to that.

Here we are assuming that you have already done your feature testing.

We are also assuming that your team is in charge of the release.

Bug Bashes

As previously stated in Chapter 8:

> *"A bug bash is a collaborative event that aims to unearth a large number of bugs within a short timebox. Bug bashes are not an exclusive testers-only event. It can involve developers, testers, product managers, designers, marketers etc."*

Source: TestProject[81]

It's important to remember here that not all "bugs" reported, are things your team will believe are bugs. Some may be enhancements. It's up to your team to decide what to do with them.

Enhancements would make your product better, but it wouldn't necessarily be problematic if they weren't implemented.

[81] https://blog.testproject.io/2021/04/05/the-ultimate-guide-to-organizing-a-bug-bash/

Why Bug Bashes Are Beneficial

Helps counter the effects of snow-blindness

Bug bashes are an effective way to gain a fresh perspective on your product/app/feature before you go live.

By being on a project (for a while), you can start to become blind to certain things.
A great way to illustrate this is that it's common for new people to discover bugs when they just join a team - this is because they have a fresh pair of eyes.

This doesn't necessarily mean that the people in the team were not testing properly. It just means that the people in the team had become blind to what it's front of them. (It's also a sign that exhaustive testing is impossible - finding *some* bugs is almost inevitable.)

You may even have very obvious bugs that are no longer obvious to the team, because the team got so used to them.

James Espie elaborates on this in a Ministry of Testing article[82]:

> *"When starting on building a feature, a team notices that their UI is slightly broken. But, as there is a workaround for the broken UI, they keep working around it.*
>
> *As time goes on though, they become so used to the workaround, that they simply stop being aware of it. The workaround becomes the norm, and they no longer 'notice' it as a problem. "*

[82]https://www.ministryoftesting.com/dojo/lessons/benefits-of-a-bug-bash-and-how-to-run-one

Learn from other people's experiences

Your team has a collection of its own experiences - by having a bug bash, your product/app/feature benefits from outside experiences.

For example: Let's say your (Profile page) team is about to release a new version of the Profile page, containing information on a user's username, email address and account activity.

Someone from the account activity team attends the bug bash.

They had problems before (in their team) with certain activities displaying correctly on other pages. Therefore, they may focus on these activities, to see if there are also problems on the Profile page.

Another advantage of having others participate is that once someone spots a problem, it can draw the team's attention to other problems that the team either previously ignored or wasn't aware of.

How To Run A Bug Bash

When to run a bug bash

- If your team does big releases, then before a release, but with enough time to fix any bugs found (i.e. 1-2 weeks before a release)
- If your team releases frequently, it's up to you. You could do one every few months to get outside feedback (and thus prevent the effects of snow-blindness).

Checklist beforehand

☐ Book a big enough room for everyone
☐ Have sent out a calendar invite to everyone, you want to attend (I suggest you send out an invite to block out 2-4 hours)
☐ If you are doing device testing, make sure devices are charged

☐ If test data needs to be set up, do that
☐ List of known bugs. (Make sure to tell participants what these are, so they don't waste time raising bugs the team is already aware of)
☐ Freeze the build - you don't want to run a bug bash on a moving target.
☐ Show everyone an example of what a good bug report looks like. (Unclear bugs create extra work for everyone)
☐ Have an overall plan of what areas need to be covered and then give people some direction based on that plan
☐ (Optional) Bring snacks for everyone

Running the Bug Bash

Now give everyone the build to test and get people set up. If people need devices to test with, give them those as well.

Make sure you are available to answer any questions that might come up during the bug bash, but if you are running the bug bash - I suggest you don't take part in the bug bash yourself.

Don't triage any bugs during the bug bash, wait until afterwards to do this.

The Release

In this section, I'll share with you some examples of how testers can be involved with releases including giving feedback on the release plan (if one exists) or helping write one as well as testing before you push to production.

> *"A simple approach to help improve a release is to have a plan for each release. A plan could involve any team members and have any kind of process."*

Source: Josh Grant, Ministry of Testing[83]

If your project doesn't already have a release plan, you can bring this up with your team and come up with one together.

Here are a few things to consider when creating a release plan:

- What does it mean to test in prod? (The important part here isn't that you make sure you have some sort of universal definition *but* that your team is on the same page here.)
- If you will run test cases, which test cases or which test suite?
- What happens if something goes wrong? Should we roll back to the previous version? If so, how would we do that?
- Does the team need to always follow the release plan? If there are exceptions, what are these exceptions? Who has the authority to make these decisions?

Depending on the project itself, your release plan will vary. A release plan for a co-located team of 3 people would probably not be suitable for a distributed team of 20 people for instance.

To give you an idea of what a release plan *might* look like, here is an example: *(Here the company chooses to have the release steps as the release plan)*

Note that Maria is a Communications Lead, Peter is a Project Manager, Anna is a Developer and Nick is a Tester.

Step Name	Description	Responsible
Have Go/No Go Meeting	Have Go/No Go meeting with affected stakeholders to decide whether the release will happen	Peter

[83]https://www.ministryoftesting.com/dojo/lessons/a-practical-guide-to-release-testing

Step Name	Description	Responsible
Send Out Comms	If the website or app needs to go down temporarily, send out marketing comms	Maria
Send out release notification	Email affected stakeholders to let them know about the release, including release details	Peter
Create release tag	Select changeset to be released to production and tag it in source control	Anna
Deploy to production	Push code to the production server for release	Anna
Release test	Test in production to ensure changes are visible in production and nothing obvious is broken	Anna and Nick

What is a Changeset?

A changeset is a formally collected set of commits that should be treated as a group, such as the commits involved in releasing a certain feature.

Source: Wikipedia[84]

[84] https://en.wikipedia.org/wiki/Changeset

Onboarding

Another advantage of a release plan is that it can be very helpful when onboarding new team members.

Having a clear release plan gives new team members an idea of what to expect.

Chapter 14: Getting Started on a Software Testing Project

Checklist for What New Testers on a Project Need

Note: your project may not include all of the below.
Make sure to check if user credentials are needed for any of the following.

☐ Access to test environments
☐ Access to instant messaging groups
☐ Added to the correct channels within the IM groups
☐ Access to the bug tracking tool
☐ Access to the test tools
☐ Access to email
☐ Team wiki
☐ Time-tracking system (applies if tester is a contractor/consultant)
☐ Version Control e.g. Git
☐ Someone to do a handover/introduction
☐ Access to the shared folders
☐ Access to the database

If you are writing test automation then the following can also be good to know/have:
☐ Access to the code repository
☐ Git branching strategy
☐ Code review process in the team
☐ Access to the CI/CD

☐ Are there already jobs created for the test automation? (or do you need to set that up)

Questions You Can Ask When You Start On a New Project

Here is a list of questions you can use to help you gain an understanding of your project and how things are run, if you are new to a project (This isn't an exhaustive list; only a starting point)

TEST ENVIRONMENTS

- How reliable are they? (this could help when it comes to raising bugs only to find they are environment issues)
- Do people's actions affect others? (how are environments shared?)
- How do you set up test environments?
- How do I know which test environment to use? (i.e. is the same one always used? does it change, how do I know it changes?)

PEOPLE

- Who do I speak to if I have questions about XXXX?
- (To buddy/mentor) who do you think I should meet?
- Who do I report to?
- Are there any testers I should meet?
- Are there any established processes they have already set up?

RAISING BUGS / HANDLING BUGS

- How do bugs get classified? (e.g. Area of Product)

- What do I do if I don't know how to classify a bug? (i.e. Is there a miscellaneous option?)
- Am I part of the bug triaging process?
- How do I help make sure that bugs are added to the sprint when needed? (i.e. Are there any particular fields I need to pay attention to here in the bug tracking tool?)
- Can you show me how to raise bugs in the bug tracking tool? (some tools need more explaining than others, especially when it comes to filling in certain fields of the system)
- Is there a bug/defect template you are expected to follow?
- If our team receives bugs from the customer or a client, what is the process for handling these? Do they have access to a bug/defect template to help them write clear reproducible bug reports?

GENERAL TESTING

- How is testing done here?
- Is there a QA process?
- Who decides how testing is done? (the tester; test lead; test manager)
- Are there any testing team meetings? (These might be outside the product team meetings – it depends on your definition of "team")
- What tests does the team currently have? (both automated and manual tests)
- What expectations does the team have when it comes to testing?
- What are people happy with when it comes to testing?
- What do you think can be improved, when it comes to testing? (being a fresh pair of eyes and ears, you're in a good position to get input from people who may not otherwise have an avenue to provide this information)

Some Final Words

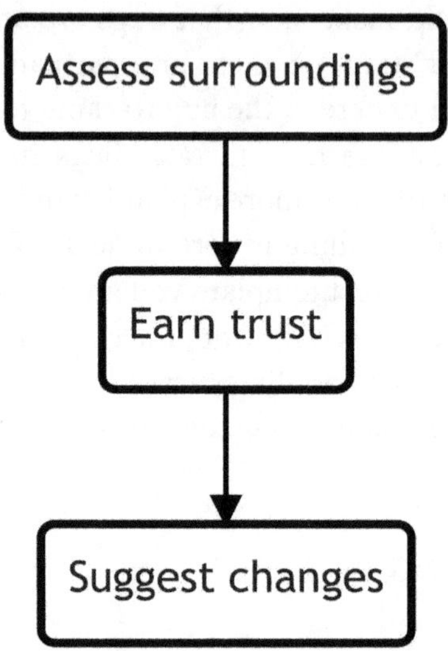

Chances are, your first few weeks will be spent getting set up, meeting people and getting to know the software you will be testing.

Depending on your project, you might not be able to do any hands-on testing for a month (or even longer).

Tip

Take detailed notes when someone shows you how to do something. Your goal should be that when someone has taught you something — you never ask them again how to do it.

Be Patient

While you may have your own opinions on how testing should be done and also how things can be improved in your new team, I would be wary of trying to change things straight away.

Take the time to get to know your surroundings and understand why things are done the way they are done.

Build rapport with your team and earn their trust. If you want to introduce some new ideas to your team, they are more likely to be receptive to it if they feel you have taken the time to understand why things are done the way they are done there.

Being too eager to do some things can run the risk of making you look naive.

How long you should wait to try and introduce new ideas also depends on the company culture. I've found some companies are very receptive to change and new ideas - while others are *very* attached to the way they do things.

An added benefit of waiting a bit before you try to change things is that you have more time to assess your surroundings and know what type of company you are at.

Is this a company that is open to new ideas?

Or is this company attached to the status quo?

Keep in mind that just because a company claims that anyone can bring forth ideas etc. this doesn't always mean this is the case.

Fresh perspective

Don't underestimate the value that a fresh perspective offers a project.

Whether this is your first testing project or your tenth, the fact that you started this project means that your team has something to learn from you.

You've got life experiences that will help you see things that others in your team might not - this will help you add value.

Ask questions.

Get to know your teammates.

Enjoy the software testing journey.

Chapter 15: Advice From Testers Around The World

Lateef Alimi, Senior Quality Assurance Analyst at Ecobank Software Center, Nigeria

1. It doesn't matter if you don't have IT experience (although I was computer literate) I used to be a bank teller. Don't feel your past experience doesn't line up with software testing.

2. It is essential to learn the basics of SQL when learning the fundamentals of software testing

3. How bugs are reported is just as important as finding the bugs themselves.

Arlene Andrews, Contract QA Engineer, USA

It takes some time to build, but having connections with all of those involved in your product makes your job as tester more complex, but also easier. Being able to talk to a decision maker helps you prove that the product is actually what the customer wants.

A friendly connection with your developers allows you add input as the code is being written, and with the official connection folks may open an opportunity to interact with the end users.

This will help you in the future to be trusted to connect to people on the many levels a tester can be of use, plus the skills built by spending time with each section of the product may identify gaps in your own knowledge.

Emna Ayadi, Testing Consultant at Sogeti France, Tunisia

Have you ever thought that one day you will travel somewhere across the world to a testing conference? Where you will be able to share your experience and challenges you face with a like minded testing community?

I see that most junior testers consider this as impossible for them; they think they need to have at least 10-20 years of experience to speak.
That's not necessarily the case, I did my very first talk in 2019, when I had only 3 years of experience.

3 simple hints to approach such a challenge:

Just start it!
Try to spot the testing activity that motivates you the most and share your personal story with the audience. Tell them how you used it in your context, how you overcame the challenges you faced. Make it unique by adding your personal story, even if it's about pairing with developers, exploring the software in new ways or any new learning that you successfully put into practice with your team.

Practice on a local level and ask for feedback
Start practicing your talk internally within your company or local communities. Nowadays, online events are much easier to reach, which means more opportunities are available.
Also ask for feedback even just a simple tweet asking for help, usually they encourage first time speakers, and everyone wants to offer their advice.

Go beyond
By having taken the first baby step, you are building a speaking history and you can definitely jump further and submit to your first international conference. Here is a good place where you can find open call for papers https://testingconferences.org[85]

Let me add an extra bonus for you, build your online reputation, share content you are passionate about on online platforms such as Twitter or LinkedIn. Try to connect with other testers that are interested in the same topics as you. With that, you will become a legend in your field and people might even reach out to you, just to learn from you, just as you reached out to others in the beginning.

Farah Chabchoub, Quality Engineering Manager at Ankorstore and Independent Quality Advisor, France

When I started my career, the most difficult thing for me was to have courage and take initiative.

With experience, I have seen that most testers face this difficulty at the start of their career. However, this act maybe the most empowering when you make your first career steps.

Proposing new testing tools or new processes shows your capacity as a fast learner. It also shows you are a critical thinker and even solution-oriented.

If you start as a tester without an engineering background do not think your job is only manual testing. Automation can be easy to implement, even without technical knowledge. Don't hesitate to handle a no-code solution that will help you in this challenge. Solutions

[85]https://testingconferences.org

like Ghost Inpector[86] for frontend testing and Runscope[87] for API testing are easy to use and would help you gain expertise gradually in the technical part by practicing development languages such as JavaScript.

Finally, the testing mission can be presented as an activity that occurs only before production deployment. Do not make this mistake and remember that testing can be done at any stage in the Software Development Lifecycle with different strategies.

You can also be involved in observability activities and use tools like Grafana[88] and Elasticsearch[89] to observe how the customers are behaving in production and highlight existing bugs that could be fixed.

Alice Chu, Test Lead at Aucerna, UK

Trust your gut instinct when testing a product or analyzing design specifications. If something feels odd or not right, always question the product. It is either a bug or deliberately designed for a reason but either way, you learn more about the application and will build up your knowledge of the product a lot quicker.

Also learn to test smarter and use your time effectively. This brings me to a tool recommendation which is one of the ways I use to save time.

Autohotkey[90] - it was recommended to me by a developer mostly used for gaming. I use it to create quick keyboard shortcuts to insert commonly used words. An example will be for testing login details which are used

---

[86] https://ghostinspector.com/
[87] https://www.runscope.com/
[88] https://grafana.com/
[89] https://www.elastic.co/
[90] https://www.autohotkey.com/

regularly during testing. A few clicks on the keyboard will type in the username or password which saves a significant amount of time if used often.

Brendan Connolly, Director of Quality Engineering at Carpe Data, USA

The best advice I can give testers is to specialize, to find a niche. Find something you are interested in that will set you apart from the perception of testers as button clickers.

One of the most straightforward and lucrative ways to specialize, that will set you up well for the future is to focus on building and testing using code. It may be intimidating at first. In addition to new skills, you will also build empathy for developers which is a powerful tool.

You may be inclined to choose automation as a specialization, but test automation is not a specific enough niche though. Automation engineers are frequently treated as a commodity very similar to how manual testers are perceived. You want to dig deeper and narrow your focus.

You want to pick a language and then stick with a stack. If you aren't sure what to choose, Javascript is the language of the browser, it is a solid choice. Learning one to two languages, where one is likely Javascript, is probably a good thing.

It's not bad to know more but learning a new programming language for a job is one thing, learning a different language for every job is another. Thrashing between languages increases some of the lag time to impact. Keep an eye on the market to stay current but as much as possible treat your knowledge in a particular language/stack as an investment and value it.

As you progress up the career ladder, you will be looked to for answers and experience beyond Selenium including things like CI/CD integration, unit testing, code coverage tools, best practices and architecture choices. By sticking with a stack you increase your time to focus on the ecosystem around the language. This allows time to get comfortable building tools, as well as tests and frameworks.

Understanding what's common, healthy and what to promote across a team adds a depth of knowledge that will propel you forward with credibility and insight. This helps you break down silos, increasing your value internally and externally. As a bonus, you increase your career options outside of "test" specific roles. If I had picked a language and stuck with a stack, I believe I would have been able to go further, more quickly and easily in my career.

Veena Davi, Lead Developer Relations at LambdaTest, India

1. Start with upskilling on debugging
Irrespective of Development, Testing, or Test Automation, debugging is one of the most crucial skills. As a QA person, understanding the error messages in UI Testing or Test Automation Code improves your bug reports and Code Quality.

I spent most of my career in Web Application Development and Testing, So I first learnt about the Chrome Developer Tools, which helps to read console logs.

2. My Suggestion on Programming Language and Tool Selection

If you have the choice of choosing your own, consider the following:

- Take top 3 current trending Programming languages,
- Give two days for each language,
- Learn from the Environment setup and choose the correct IDE
- Work on basic concepts like understanding variables and functions.

I did nine days of research. I tried Java (Eclipse), C# (Visual Studio) and JavaScript (Visual Studio Code) and am now much into Java with Eclipse.

Having the proper purpose pushes you to learn and master that skill; contributing to Open Source in the initial stages of your career is one of the best ways to get your hands dirty with coding

I chose "Knowledge Sharing" as my way of nurturing my learnings.

There are a lot of platforms like blogs, meet-ups, seminars and conferences. Every individual is unique - so select the way you enjoy reaching your goal.

Learn - Share - Grow Together

Adebayo Jacobs-Amoo (Tea Pot), Software Testing Manager, Co-Founder of The Test Chat Community (TTC), UK

Not getting adequate support
Most freshers looking to come into software testing are seeking helpers instead of seeking help. They target a set of people, who they think might be able to help them, and when that help is not forthcoming, they often get disappointed, most people give up and look to do

something else. These highly sought-after people might be quite busy, with not enough time to mentor others.

Inaccessibility to accurate information
There are many people out there peddling inaccurate information about what testing is and what freshers should do to be successful at testing. Most of the peddlers are just after making some money, often talk about popular topics in testing that a lot of freshers have heard about.

One-sided Knowledge
All the freshers we have come across in the past 2 years knew about automation, they believe if they know how to use a tool, they are good to go, this is a wrong approach to becoming a software tester. One need to first understand the fundamentals of testing, before learning how to use an assistant (test tools) It is not a one size fit all.

Forming the Test Chat Community (TTC)
Introducing The Test Chat Community (TTC); a professional support system for software testers. Our objective is to provide accurate information to everyone and propagate the knowledge in a way people understand why we do what we do. We have people like James Bach, Michael Bolton, Brijesh Deb (the Leader of the community) and a host of other software testing professionals.

We encourage anyone who wants to become a tester to be confident, bold, and active. A lot of the members dedicate their time to teaching testers (freshers and experienced alike) to educate others about testing.

In the community, everyone learns from the experiences of other members by simply sharing, so there is no lead teacher.

We encourage members to participate by merely asking

questions and sharing additional contributions to any conversation. Conversations are triggered by questions in the group and usually results in webinars, blogs and courses designed on the back of the conversation.

We provide an avenue for freshers and experienced people to directly engage with people they might otherwise not be able to reach.

I became a Test Manager in 2006 but I have learnt so much from The Test Chat Community (TTC), and from the conversations in the group.

Recently, a fresher who had a one-on-one conversation with James Bach in preparation for his job interview, felt he made a fool of himself by asking questions and getting tutored openly, but the community encouraged him and shared more information with him for his interview. Few days later, he informed the community that he got the job, and his employer was amazed at how much he knew about testing.

We published an eBook last year titled 21Days21Tips for Software testers. The book is available for download via our LinkedIn Page.

We are active on Telegram, LinkedIn, Twitter, and Facebook; we are known as The Test Chat Community (TTC). Our YouTube Channel[91] is a valuable resource freely available to everyone, to learn first-hand from experienced software testing professionals.

I strongly recommend all prospective software testers to find communities like The Test Chat Community (TTC), join and become active in them.

Sylvia Killinen, Security Engineer, USA

[91] https://www.youtube.com/c/TheTestChat

You can learn as much in security testing as you're inclined to - it's a specialization with both depth (within a technology or system) and breadth (across many technologies and systems).

The learning curve can be intense, but the need for secure systems has never been greater.

If you want to test the security of a system, threat modeling and practical testing go hand in hand. Threat modeling is a way of understanding how an attacker might misuse a system; practical security testing is trying to misuse it yourself in a safe environment, and recording how and why it fails.

It's very effective to start with understanding what you're trying to protect. Is it data, a function that shouldn't be accessed by just anyone, a resource of some type?

Once you have that, you can move on to how it's supposed to be accessed, and how it can be accessed without going through the desired path.

In general, the more understanding you have about how the technology actually works, the easier your process of security testing will be. Begin there, and see where this path takes you.

Beth Marshall, QA Rel at Mailinator, UK

People looking to get into testing often find themselves in a Catch 22 situation, where companies struggle to hire testers without experience, but there seems to be little way of getting experience without getting a job first. Sound familiar?

As someone who grew up in a pretty economically deprived town on the east coast of the UK, and who only ever had low paid jobs until they stumbled into Tech, I think it is incredibly exciting just how much we can learn for free if we want to - all from the comfort of our own bedrooms.

One way of leveraging this concept, that could directly lead you to landing that first role in QA, is the idea of Test Portfolios.

A test portfolio can be something as simple as a free Trello board or linktr.ee where you bookmark all the interesting things you want to learn or try out and pop some evidence in when they're done.

One of the QA's at my previous company did a testing bootcamp and created a test portfolio as part of that (in the form of a Trello board) to help them land their first role.

They showed this portfolio to their prospective employer and they were blown away - I know that because I was the person who showed it to them. I wanted to persuade my boss to hire the company's first Junior QA.

The fact this person had knowledge of where to find answers to their questions, an appetite for learning more about testing and evidence of what they had done made the difference between a yes and a "not yet".

In creating and showing off your portfolio, you are helping your future employers to mentally derisk you as a new hire. Plus you've learned a tonne in the process - win win!

The other good thing about a portfolio is this - it is completely up to you what to put in it. Perhaps you want to add a few Test Automation University certificates (free), or maybe add comments against a Testing podcast that you listened to about what it taught you (also free) or maybe learn about the different types of test methods, see which one you're drawn to and evidence your learning there (guess what, thats free too). The only commitment is your time.

Gaston Marichal, QA Lead at QAlified, Uruguay

When testing, I like to think I'm experimenting and I treat the product as an a unstable piece of software. I think of different combinations of values, flows and conditions cause this is what real user would do.

I like to think the software as a box that receive inputs, process those inputs and give some response back. So, those inputs, their different values, combinations and even the order will affect the way that the box process and the results also.

Cecelia Martinez, Quality Advisor, USA

Ask about and understand the relationship between the testing and development teams. How collaborative? How do their workflows overlap? How easy is it to communicate? Is there mutual respect? Ask managers then colleagues and see if the answers are consistent.

Laveena Ramchandani, Testing & Quality Assurance Lead at EasyJet, UK

I have been in the testing industry for nine years now, it has been a great ride for me as I fell into testing and did not know how many things one can learn as a software tester.

I see testing as a great role because it's a great mix between technical and non-technical knowledge. I have also seen a switch from the traditional testing mindset to a new way of thinking and being part of a community.

As a tester in your early days, make sure you join as many communities and learn or even be part of their events too!

Some advice to new testers or testers in their early days:

Be open to opportunities –
There is so much to learn, so why not learn new ways of testing, or new techniques, collaborate with other testers or even members within your team like a UX designer or a developer?

Be open to challenges
Challenges can be nerve wracking, but if you think about it in a positive way you can learn so many things out of it. For instance, I was questioned about an incident that happened in a live environment I was worried at the start what did I do wrong when testing? But it was not down to me it was a team effort to resolve this. Sometimes I find when you are thrown with challenges, take them gracefully as you never know what you will discover.

Enhance your testing skills
Keep up to date with trends in testing. I really enjoyed talks at conferences around accessibility and I started bringing accessibility into my team and other teams. This was taken positively, and great changes came with it. Automation is another area I really like to stay up to date with and would advice to a new tester to look into this too and learn which tool is right for you. For me I found Cypress the right match as I could work with Javascript and my application was more front end focused. I like Cypress too because the ease in using the framework, the community and there is so much

material about it. It is important to understand what automation is, how can it be achieved and all of the hard work that goes into it from the very start till the time an automation test suite is ready. Also, it's good to focus on maintaining the automation tests making sure its bringing value and quality.

Try new things
You cannot make a good decision until you have tried it. There is so much support out there. Network; socialise; collaborate with individuals. You never know how a small chat can do wonders for you. There is always something that's a best fit for you, think of the world as a puzzle, you will fit somewhere and feel good about it.

Learn, collaborate, share & succeed.

Xavi Ametller Serrat, Software Developer at Criteo, Spain

Being a Software tester is a demanding and rewarding role. To be successful at it my recommendation is that, first of all, you should understand Software Development as a holistic practice, with testing being a part of it. Look for companies who value that activity as a first class citizen.

On a personal level, I recommend you to consciously work on various skill sets:

Testing techniques
What worked for me in my early days was to start studying multiple techniques. Having knowledge and awareness of a wide breadth of techniques gave me the resources to tackle multiple problems, usually mixing and matching strategies.

Relationships
Software Development is always a social activity, so

we have to be good at socializing. Distilling what's important, reading the room, knowing who and how to ask are very important assets, especially when part of your work is to pin-point things that are not working as expected.

Outside of your work socializing is also important, lean on the community (meetups, conferences, Twitter) to learn and network.

Automation
The trend in SW development towards Continuous Delivery and DevOps leads us to a position where we want to release continuously. Releasing often and with a sustainable pace requires good test automation (or lots of boldness).

You can be a good tester if you don't automate (as long as the team helps on that), but the ability to understand, tweak, adapt, or even create your own code is like having super powers worth investing in.

Domain
Probably the less portable of your learnings but a tester who doesn't understand its domain will hardly be able to make sensible contributions to the product. Since you'll have to go deep, find a domain you like (it will be much more fun).

Shawn Shaligram, Quality Engineer ICM at Lyft Inc, USA

I'd encourage testers new to the industry to study and explore their bugs via 'the process of elimination' - did we introduce it recently or is it legacy? Is it configuration related? Device specific etc? Does it behave the same way on android as it does on iOS ?

Spending more time identifying the root cause can help devs fix it faster but also help testers identify risk areas and develop a set of heuristics that can help detect more bugs within a short timeframe.

Ken Simeon, QA Manager at RippleMatch, USA

Don't fall into the trap of being in a perpetual cycle of wanting to do or wanting to be something. Instead be in a perpetual cycle of learning something new and applying it.

Throughout my career as a hiring manager, I've heard countless times that a candidate wants to learn automation or be an automation engineer.

I immediately ask, what are you doing to get there? And how long have you been on this journey?

The majority of responses have been something like, I've been learning about (insert popular test automation framework here) because that is what's used at work. I've been learning it on & off for the past few years because I don't get enough time at work.

As a result, hiring managers could jump to one of the following conclusions:

1. If they're not doing it, they don't have the aptitude to do it.
2. This person really isn't learning about automation.
3. This person is not a fast learner.

Being in a perpetual cycle of wanting & not doing will leave any professional in a decelerated career path. The only way not to be on a flat or slow career path is to put in the extra time to learn new skills.

The approach I've used to aid those that want to learn automated testing is that they need to learn the foundations of the language used in their automation framework of choice and beyond the basics of the technology they want to automate.

For instance, you're a QA professional wanting to write automated tests for a web application using a JavaScript framework and Selenium.

The directions I've advised individuals to take is the following;

- Learn HTML & CSS to the point you can create yourself a working stylized web site.
- Learn the advanced foundations of the JavasScript language and apply them to your website.
- Learn about the framework & the underlying technology that enabled the automation (ie. Selenium Webdriver).
- Learn about the fundamentals of unit testing.
- Put all the pieces together behind a solid goal of automating a single functional area of a feature before expanding beyond that scope.

When QA professionals hear this suggestion, they can be discouraged by the magnitude of knowledge and the time it could take to consume & apply the knowledge.

But that is the point.

Advancing one's knowledge and career takes time & effort. None of it is just handed to a person. Those that truly have the goal will find the time and put in the effort.

There are those that wil try to find a shortcut. Thst is ok as long as they are continuing to learn & applying the knowledge they've gained.

How does the breakdown of these various areas of learning apply to both a QA professional's current career and their goal of becoming an automation engineer?

Learning HTML & CSS gives the individual a foundation of how a website is put together. It will aid in the conversations with developers, UX designers and product managers around the customer experience.

It will also help with the explanation of issues with a web experience to a developer and provide the foundational information that accelerates a potential fix.

Learning JavaScript for a web page helps a QA professional understand how interactions can happen on a web page. They will also learn how to troubleshoot and debug issues.

This directly applies back to their current role by allowing them to give more detailed information to a developer when an issue is experienced.

Learning beyond the foundations of a programming language is key. Without this, one won't know or understand how to structure their code base. They won't fully understand why automation frameworks work or behave in a certain way.

Beyond that, it will give a person an overall foundation behind programming in general. This aids in your conversations in your profession. Now your conversations with developers & technical leaders will shift.

You'll begin understanding how all the inner parts of the code work together and be able to ask technical questions that could drive deeper conversations & understanding for a better user experience.

The key to learning about Unit Testing, is that not all automated tests from a QA organization should be End-to-End test scenarios. End-to-End tests do have their place within an automated test suite, but that's not the end all be all.

Finally when you put all of the learnings together, there

is a knowledgeable approach already gained by the QA Professional and along the journey they've been leveraging their knowledge in their daily job.

This leveraging of knowledge in your job function is the primary key to showing self progression and will lead to accelerated professional progression within your company.

Mohamed Tarek, Software Testing Expert at DXC Technology, Egypt

General Advice

- Stay in a company as long as you learn something new.
- Your loyalty should be to your career more than to your current company.

Technical Advice

- Be aware of the non-functional testing side of software testing, it may be hard in the beginning to have a role as non-functional tester but it will give a wider vision about the software industry.
- Attend technical meet-ups (OWASP Chapters, Ministry of Testing) and play with open source tools (OWASP Zap, Apache JMeter, Gatling)
- You can ask to run some non-functional tests aside your daily tasks , I know this will be an extra work but it will be a great opportunity to play with these tools in a safe environment.

About the Author

Nicola Lindgren is a Senior QA Engineer/ QA Manager, based in Malmö, Sweden. She is an international conference speaker, frequent blogger and avid learner of all things testing, agile and leadership.

She has worked on projects in a wide range of industries including Trade, Education, Payments, e-Commerce, Transport and Gaming. She has worked in Agile (Scrum, Kanban), Continuous Delivery and Waterfall environments, in both co-located and distributed teams.

Nicola started two testing meetups (one in Auckland, New Zealand and one in Stockholm, Sweden), has taught software testing courses and run workshops, coached and mentored multiple testers and written for various testing publications. She has also been a co-intructor for the BBST Foundations course multiple times.

You can find Nicola on Twitter[92] or LinkedIn[93].

She blogs about testing, automation, personal development and agile at nicolalindgren.com[94]

[92]https://twitter.com/NicolaLindgren
[93]https://www.linkedin.com/in/nicolalindgren/
[94]https://nicolalindgren.com/

Recommended Reading

Conferences for Networking:

- Here you can find a list of Developer Conferences[95]
- Here you can find a list of Software Testing Conferences[96]

General Testing:

- Cognitive Biases in Software Testing[97]
- Essentials - Introduction to Software Development and Testing[98]
- The Whole Team Approach to Continuous Testing[99]
- Elizabeth Hendrickson's Test Heuristics Cheat Sheet[100]

Writing Effective Bug Reports

- Rapid Software Testing Guide to Bug Reporting[101]
- The Art of the Bug Report[102]

Learn Test Automation (courses):

- Android Test Automation with Espresso[103]

[95] https://dev.events/
[96] https://testingconferences.org/
[97] https://www.ministryoftesting.com/dojo/courses/cognitive-biases-in-software-testing
[98] https://www.ministryoftesting.com/dojo/courses/essentials-introduction-to-software-development-and-testing
[99] https://testautomationu.applitools.com/the-whole-team-approach-to-continuous-testing/
[100] https://testobsessed.com/wp-content/uploads/2011/04/testheuristicscheatsheetv1.pdf
[101] https://www.satisfice.com/download/rapid-testing-guide-to-making-good-bug-reports
[102] https://www.ministryoftesting.com/dojo/lessons/the-art-of-the-bug-report
[103] https://testautomationu.applitools.com/espresso-mobile-testing-tutorial/

- Source Control for Test Automation with Git[104]
- IntelliJ for Test Automation Engineers[105]
- Selenium Webdriver with Java[106]
- Java Programming[107]
- Introduction to iOS Test Automation with XCUITest[108]
- Exploring Service APIs through Test Automation[109]
- A Software Tester's Guide to Chrome Dev Tools[110]

Learn Test Automation (demo sites):

- Discussion Thread where people share various sites you can practice test automation[111]
- Want to practice Test Automation? Try these Demo Sites! by Andrew Knight[112]
- 19 Websites to Practice Automation Testing (UI, API, Mobile) by Nikolay Advolodkin[113]
- Best Demo Websites for Practicing Different Types of Software Tests by Federico Toledo[114]

Some of my favourite blog posts and articles on how to write better test automation:

- Are Automated Retries Good or Bad? By Andrew Knight[115]

[104]https://testautomationu.applitools.com/git-tutorial/

[105]https://testautomationu.applitools.com/intellij/

[106]https://testautomationu.applitools.com/selenium-webdriver-tutorial-java/

[107]https://testautomationu.applitools.com/selenium-webdriver-tutorial-java/

[108]https://testautomationu.applitools.com/introduction-to-ios-test-automation-with-xcuitest/

[109]https://testautomationu.applitools.com/exploring-service-apis-through-test-automation/

[110]https://www.ministryoftesting.com/dojo/courses/a-software-tester-s-guide-to-chrome-devtools

[111]https://club.ministryoftesting.com/t/products-and-sites-to-practice-testing-on/1242/5

[112]https://automationpanda.com/2021/12/29/want-to-practice-test-automation-try-these-demo-sites/

[113]https://ultimateqa.com/dummy-automation-websites/

[114]https://abstracta.us/blog/software-testing/best-demo-websites-for-practicing-different-types-of-software-tests/

[115]https://automationpanda.com/2021/06/14/are-automated-test-retries-good-or-bad/

- In Search of a Test Automation Strategy by Maaret Pyhäjärvi[116]
- What To Consider When Doing Visual Testing by Marie Drake[117]
- Tips for Healthy Page Object Classes by Angie Jones[118]
- Do you really need that Cucumber with your Selenium? by Bas Dijkstra[119]
- TRIMS - A Mnemonic for Valuable Automation in Testing by Richard Bradshaw[120]

Learn how to do Exploratory Testing:

- The Exploratory Testing Week 2021 series[121]

Most of the videos in this series can be viewed with a free membership.

- Exploratory Testing on Computer Interfaces(APIs) by Maaret Pyhäjärvi[122]

Unlike most online resources/videos about Exploratory Testing that focus on the user interface, this talk focusses on the API level.

- Rapid Software Testing Course[123]

---

[116]https://visible-quality.blogspot.com/2021/02/in-search-of-test-automation-strategy.html?m=1

[117]https://www.mariedrake.com/post/what-to-consider-when-doing-visual-testing

[118]https://angiejones.tech/page-object-model/

[119]https://www.ontestautomation.com/do-you-really-need-that-cucumber-with-your-selenium/

[120]https://automationintesting.com/2019/08/trims-automation-in-testing-strategy.html

[121]https://www.ministryoftesting.com/dojo/series/exploratory-testing-week-2021/lessons/experience-report-risks-and-charters-with-simon-tomes

[122]https://www.youtube.com/watch?v=Wh3MTHyA1tQ&ab_channel=ServerlessArchitectureConference

[123]https://rapid-software-testing.com/attending-rst/

Everyone I know who has taken this course has spoken very highly about it.

- Explore It! by Elizabeth Hendrickson[124]

Great book on how to do exploratory testing

- Ministry of Testing Podcast - Exploratory Testing Panel[125]

One of the hosts interviews me and two other experts, Dave Harrison and Callum Akehurst-Ryan, about exploratory testing.

- Reporting Session Based Testing[126]

This post by Katrina Clokie explains how her team reported session based testing (SBTM).

- Exploratory Testing Academy[127]

*A site created in collaboration between a seasoned tester (Maaret Pyhäjärvi) and a newbie tester (Mirja Pyhäjärvi), that shows you how to do exploratory testing.

Testability

- Testability Advocacy Canvas[128]

A tool for supporting you in becoming testability advocates, created by Ash Winter.

---

[124]https://pragprog.com/titles/ehxta/explore-it/

[125](https://www.ministryoftesting.com/dojo/lessons/mot-podcast-exploratory-testing-panel)

[126]http://katrinatester.blogspot.com/2014/03/reporting-session-based-testing.html

[127]https://www.exploratorytestingacademy.com/

[128]https://diagramindustries.com/2021/12/15/testability-advocacy-canvas/

- Dimensions of Testability[129]

Model by Maria Kedemo and Ben Kelly

- Testability Sales Pitch[130]

By Ash Winter

- Team Guide to Software Testability[131]

Book by Ash Winter and Rob Meaney offering practical insights on testability

- Testability of Requirements[132]

Useful resource by Ranorex on Testability of requirements

Software Testing Online Forums:

- Ministry for Testing - The Club[133]
- EuroSTAR Huddle[134]

Job Hunting Resources

- How To Interview Like A Tester by Elizabeth Zagroba[135]

A lot of useful tips for interviewing for roles

[129]https://mkedemo.wordpress.com/2015/11/22/dimensions-of-testability-v1-1/
[130]https://www.slideshare.net/AshWinter/testability-sales-pitch-232256929
[131]https://leanpub.com/softwaretestability
[132]https://www.ranorex.com/blog/10-best-practices-8-write-testable-requirements/
[133]https://club.ministryoftesting.com/
[134]https://huddle.eurostarsoftwaretesting.com/topics/
[135]https://www.ministryoftesting.com/dojo/lessons/how-to-interview-like-a-tester?s_id=12232999

- Reverse Interview Github Repository[136]

List of questions to ask a potential employer at an interview - this list is targeted at developers but most of questions would apply to a testing role as well.

- Randall Kanna's Ultimate List of Job Sites for Developers[137]

While a lot of these sites are targeted tha developers, there are many that would be useful for testers as well.

- Ministry of Testing's Job Board[138]

Jobs posted are mainly for the UK and the USA, but there are a few posted for elsewhere.

- Zipjob free review[139]

You can get a free review on your resume within 48 hours. Keep in mind this seems to be targeted at the US market.

YouTube Channels

- Sam Connelly's YouTube channel[140]

If you want to see what testing looks like, Sam's channel is a great one to check out - she pairs with other testers and you get to hear their thought process.

- Software Testing by Daniel Knott[141]

[136] https://github.com/viraptor/reverse-interview
[137] https://randallkanna.com/job-sites-for-developers/
[138] https://www.ministryoftesting.com/jobs
[139] https://www.zipjob.com/free-review/
[140] https://www.youtube.com/c/SamConnelly
[141] https://www.youtube.com/c/DanielKnott

A wide range of topics is covered including how to get started in testing, mobile testing tips and opinions on certification.

- The Test Chat[142]

Various testers share their experiences and give tips on how to apply different techniques etc.

- Whiteboard Testing[143]

Not currently being updated (last video was from August 2019), but still a great resource for learning various concepts such as Integration Testing and the Test Pyramid.

Miscellaneous

- 10 Usability Heuristics for User Interface Design[144]
- Philosophe.com[145]

A site that explores the relationship between testing and quality.

- The four-hour tester[146]

This site has exercises that help you identify transferrable skills you might have, which would be useful in testing.

- Workroom Productions[147]

James Lindsay has some great videos here explaining key concepts such as Feedback and Session-based testing.

[142]https://www.youtube.com/c/TheTestChat/featured
[143]https://www.youtube.com/c/WhiteboardTesting
[144]https://www.nngroup.com/articles/ten-usability-heuristics/
[145]https://www.philosophe.com/
[146]https://www.fourhourtester.net/
[147]https://vimeo.com/workroomprds

Notes

Chapter 1: What is Software Testing? And Other Definitions

Chapter 2: Gaining Skills Before (And After) Your First Role

Chapter 3: Getting Your First Job As A Software Tester

Chapter 5: How and Why You Should Find a Mentor

Chapter 6: What I Wish I Knew in My First Year of Testing

Chapter 7: Bug Reports

Chapter 8: Test Cases vs Exploratory Testing vs Ad Hoc Testing

Chapter 9: Testing Against Implicit Requirements

Chapter 10: Test Automation

Chapter 11: How To Prevent Bugs

Chapter 12: Ask For Testability

Chapter 13: Preparing For Releases

Chapter 15: Advice From Testers Around The World

About the Author

www.ingramcontent.com/pod-product-compliance
Lightning Source LLC
LaVergne TN
LVHW010552160826
845677LV00013B/3105
* 9 7 8 9 1 5 2 7 2 6 8 5 3 *